PARKER HOMESTEAD

PARKER HOMESTEAD

· A History and Guide ·

Mary Anne Parker

Published by The History Press
Charleston, SC 29403
www.historypress.net

Copyright © 2013 by Mary Anne Parker
All rights reserved

Back cover, top right: Family photo by Nikki Morrow.

First published 2013

Manufactured in the United States

ISBN 978.1.62619.273.7

Library of Congress CIP data applied for.

Notice: The information in this book is true and complete to the best of our knowledge. It is offered without guarantee on the part of the author or The History Press. The author and The History Press disclaim all liability in connection with the use of this book.

All rights reserved. No part of this book may be reproduced or transmitted in any form whatsoever without prior written permission from the publisher except in the case of brief quotations embodied in critical articles and reviews.

CONTENTS

Foreword, by Teressa Parker   7
Acknowledgements   9
Introduction   11
Background   13

1. Parker Homestead's Beginning: Clark's Cabin   15
2. The First Field Trips   21
3. Phil: His Great Sorghum Adventure and the First Festival   27
4. The Aftermath of the First Sorghum Cookin'   41
5. The Three Parker Homestead Barns   47
6. The Post Office and Print Shop   55
7. Roberts Chapel   61
8. The General Store   69
9. The Broom Shops   77
10. The Smokehouse and Picnic Area   87
11. The Kettle Corn Shed   93
12. The Blacksmith Shop, the Sarsaparilla Shed and Julie Bell's Barn   99
13. The Gristmill   105
14. The E. Sloan Heritage School   111
15. The Johnson House, Way Station, Brush Arbor and Covered Bridge   119

Contents

16. Bee Branch and Tony's 'Tiques	125
17. The Foust House	133
18. Parker Homestead Honorable Mention: The Bacon Hotel	141
19. The Outtakes	147
Index	153
About the Author	157

FOREWORD

In helping Mary Anne with this history of the Homestead, I began to realize anew just how much of our lives have been spent "out back." Over the years, I have always said this must be God's purpose for us in life—it came together too easily. We never sat down and said, "Let's build a Homestead!" It just happened. Even though the work was hard, especially when we were putting up log buildings, everything seemed to fall into place almost in spite of us. If we needed something, it appeared (even if we didn't know it was needed).

Many of the artifacts have journeyed a long way only to find their way back home to Whitehall. For every building we built, there were enough items to completely furnish it by the time we were finished with construction, thanks to people donating items or telling us where to find them. If we didn't know how to do something, someone would come along who did. We inadvertently became the curators of the collective memories of everyone involved in some way, both large and small. I can't tell you how many visitors begin their conversations with, "I remember when…"

We were young and tireless and nobody told us it couldn't be done. Oh, there were a few naysayers in the beginning. When we first talked about starting a festival, a good friend told us, "Nobody's going to come all the way out here to Whitehall; I just don't think they will." Well as the saying goes, we built it, and they did come. It's turned into something bigger than we are, a place for everybody—young and old—to enjoy. More than one person has told us they feel a sense of peace when they step onto the grounds, shedding their everyday worries and hassles.

Foreword

We share an intangible ownership of the Homestead with all the remarkable people we have met on our journey. In fact, so many people that I'm sure we have not mentioned them all in this book. And for any oversight, I can assure you it's unintentional. We began this adventure almost thirty years ago, and many things, especially from the beginning, have become fuzzy. Mary Anne would ask us a specific question about something early on, and Phil and I would both look at her with a blank stare and shrug or shake our heads. But the big picture remains the same: we could not have done this without the help and support of numerous family members and friends. Our extended Homestead family continues to grow, and we look forward to many more years of "Homestead Moments" with all of you.

Teressa Parker
Parker Homestead

ACKNOWLEDGEMENTS

This book has been such a joy to write. I have had the pleasure of sitting with my in-laws and furiously jotting things down as they relived all sorts of memories I might never have known about otherwise. I am very thankful that together as a family we now have a written record to share with our friends, family, visitors and the future generations who will come to love Parker Homestead as we do.

I have written this with our many, many Homestead volunteers and friends we have made over the years in mind. We are so thankful for the friends we have, the friends who have since passed away and the legacies they all have left behind. We are also thankful for the opportunity to educate thousands of students and visitors each year about Whitehall history, Arkansas history and our little place.

The Homestead has accomplished so many things it is hard for most to choose their favorite thing about it. For me it is simple: the Homestead is where I fell in love with my husband, Cy, who at twenty years old took a chance on a single woman with a young daughter and never thought twice about giving us both his name a few years later. We fell in love and married at the Homestead and now choose to raise our children here on the grounds—the place he grew up. We are fortunate to make our home surrounded by cabins Cy built with his dad and granddad, and we are proud to see our children now working at the Homestead beside their father, Grammy and Phil Daddy.

So to all of the family and friends who have supported us, sweated and worked with us, laughed and cried with us, we thank you. And to my husband, Cyboy, this book is for you.

INTRODUCTION

Once upon a time, about 150 years ago, old man Parker moved his wife and six children, their mule, wagon and all their belongings to an area off Crowley's Ridge that wasn't yet named. The area that would come to be known as Whitehall was a wild, impenetrable forest at that time, but old man Parker saw opportunity. He set about clearing land and building log cabins, and before too long, the area became known as Parker Homestead.

Just kidding.

The above story is only one of the tales of Parker Homestead's origin I have heard over the years. The story has many variations. I once overheard a bus driver at our annual field trips telling a visiting parent, "I used to play out here on Parker's Plantation when I was a kid. Old man Parker was well to do, and at that time, all of these cabins were really something."

I listened in disbelief. And even though I tried to tell the bus driver that none of these cabins were here when he was a kid—as a matter of fact, none were here at all until the mid-1980s—he would have no part of it. He had a good story, and he was sticking to it.

When Phil and Teressa Parker, owners of Parker Homestead, were in their forties and doing broom-making demonstrations for field trips, they were often asked, "What ever happened to Mr. and Mrs. Parker? Are they even still alive?" Another popular question they received was "Did this place belong to your grandparents?" The students and teachers asking them had no idea that the Mr. and Mrs. Parker they were referring to—the original founders of the Homestead—were right in front of them. Once Phil and

Introduction

Teressa told them the truth, astonishment would show on their faces. They could hardly believe it.

But sometimes the truth is even stranger and more wonderful than fiction.

I am so excited to share with you all the real story of Parker Homestead. I have struggled with whether to relay it chronologically, which is the only way that makes sense to us, or cabin by cabin, which would be the only way that would make sense as a reference for you. So please excuse me if I do a little of both.

I am going to start at the beginning and then walk you through the Homestead cabin by cabin the best I can, while including some family stories and dynamics, a few good recipes and some pioneer tips, tricks and lore. So welcome to the real story of Parker Homestead, a tale of hard work and accidental good fortune, of Arkansas history and of our wonderful friends and family who helped along the way. We hope you enjoy the journey as much as we have.

BACKGROUND

Parker Homestead is a magnificent place, built piece by piece by Phil and Teressa Parker; their son, Cy; Phil's father, Bob; and numerous friends and family members over a twenty-year period. Building the Homestead has not been easy, but Teressa says, "We have been truly blessed with the people we have met and friends we have made along the way—people we would never have known without the Homestead. In fact, there is a rather large 'Homestead family,' as we call it, which includes everyone who has been a part of this journey through the years. They feel a sense of ownership with us."

Many of the Homestead's first cabins and artifacts came from in and around Whitehall, the small community six miles south of Harrisburg where the Homestead sits. Whitehall has a very rich history, one that local residents were quite fond of, and for that reason, it seemed that all of them had stashed away a thing or two from Whitehall's past. Though locals didn't really have any reason to cubbyhole artifacts, many of them just felt like they should save their memories in some concrete way, even if it were just by keeping something in their closet or storage building or sharing the stories of their past and adventures with their children.

Whitehall was first named White Hall, but because of the existence of another town in Arkansas by the same name, the Poinsett County community changed its name to Whitehall. The original road into Whitehall was the Old Military Road, which runs behind Homestead creek. The first post office in Whitehall was opened in 1882, which coordinated with the laying of the St. Louis and Iron Mountain Railway tracks. With the railroad in place, large logging companies from up north began to clear-cut and haul out lumber by train. Then, in 1912, Mr. E.A. Gilbert purchased and laid out Gilbert's division in Whitehall. He set up lots, roads and a town plan. I have the original plan framed and hanging in my kitchen.

Also in 1912, Mr. James William Bacon bought Lot 4, Block 4 of Gilbert's division. Sitting there, on the front of my property, is the Bacon Hotel. Carved into its steps are the words "Bacon Hotel, White Hall, Ark., May 30, 1912."

Whitehall had more going on than a post office, a railroad, a hotel and a name change. There were several stores, a gristmill, a stockyard, a school, a sawmill, a depot and a large orchard. As often happens in small rural communities, the school was consolidated with a larger one nearby, and students were bused to Harrisburg. The post office was closed as well. As children of Whitehall grew up, they started to drive other places to look for work, and many moved off. The remnants of this thriving small community still stand, but all the stores and businesses have now been closed. Residents with strong ties to these businesses kept mementos that, over the years, simply began to gather dust. And then in 1984, Phil Parker decided to move a small log cabin into his backyard and set it up right across the creek from the Old Military Road, the original road into Whitehall.

1
PARKER HOMESTEAD'S BEGINNING

Clark's Cabin

In 1984, Phil and Teresa Parker were a young couple with two small children living in Whitehall, Arkansas. They weren't unlike their neighbors, working and raising kids. Phil was a bricklayer in Memphis, and Teressa was a first grade teacher in nearby Harrisburg.

It was about this time, that Phil heard Mr. Bruce Clark was going to burn down an old log cabin. Phil went to Brown's grocery in Whitehall looking for Mr. Clark and asked Clark if he could tear down the cabin and have it if he cleaned up the land afterward. Mr. Clark said that was fine, and Phil set about the task.

Phil and Teressa's house backed up to some woods, and Phil thought that would be the perfect place to set up the cabin. After Clark's cabin was moved and set up, Phil and Teressa had friends over to play cards, have parties and other activities in the little cabin in their backyard.

Clark's Cabin was originally a two-room dwelling built during the Depression, though Phil was only able to salvage enough to make it into a one-room cabin. The Parkers were proud of their little hangout and set about to furnish it as best they could. They got an old rope bed with a hay mattress from Teressa's uncle C. Edward Tudor, some kerosene lamps, a few cane-backed chairs, some rockers and old photographs. When they were done, it was easy to believe walking into Clark's Cabin that you were entering someone's house from long ago, someone who was out working but set to come back in from the fields any time for supper.

The spot became quite popular, and Phil and Teressa decided to add a few more things. An old family barn that once belonged to Teressa's great-

The inside of Clark's Cabin, circa 1985. *Parker Family Collection.*

Teressa's grandpa Dode Heeb's wagon, pictured at the Homestead, circa mid-1980s. *Parker Family Collection.*

grandpa August Heeb fell over around this time. Phil and Teressa asked if it was all right to salvage some lumber from it to make an outhouse with. The reclaimed-wood outhouse was a nice addition to the side of Clark's Cabin and a big hit with everyone who saw it.

So many things happened at once—and seemingly by accident or design—that led the little hangout in the backyard to turn into something more. Teressa's grandpa Alfred "Dode" Heeb had set out several years before to build himself a covered wagon. Dode was an avid collector of interesting things and had a working knowledge of how to build a wagon, so he combed through all kinds of sales, flea markets and junk stores until he had all the metal parts necessary to build it. Though the wagon wasn't an authentic family wagon, it was something to behold. Dode treasured it, and after his death in 1989, Teressa's grandma Berneda Nix Heeb gave the wagon to Phil and Teressa.

> **A Pioneer Fruit Tip**
>
> When picking blackberries, soak a string in coal oil and tie it around your ankle. That way, the chiggers and other no-see-ums won't get you. All the students and teachers in attendance for a field trip one year probably wished they had known this. The hay bales used for seating that year were full of chiggers. One teacher had to see a doctor because the chiggers on her posterior were so bad.

So now Phil's little hangout had a log cabin, an outhouse and a covered wagon, and yet they wanted more. Phil knew about an old cabin up on Hill Street in Harrisburg, and he knew that he would really like to have it. The small one-room cabin was built in 1924 by Jesse Brunson as a home for his family of five. Phil contacted Lucille Brunson Shannon and asked about buying it. She agreed, and a price was set of fifty dollars.

Phil tore it down and brought it to his backyard with the intention of attaching it to the back of Clark's Cabin, separated by a small breezeway, to make a dogtrot building. But once Phil returned home with the cabin, he received a call from Ms. Shannon. She informed him that the price of fifty dollars was for the logs—that price did not include the floor, the tin and everything else attached to the building that Phil had taken. Phil was taken aback, apologized and drove back to Harrisburg to pay Ms. Shannon an additional fifty dollars.

After the dogtrot addition was set up, the Parkers went about setting up the old Brunson residence as a kitchen. Mr. and Mrs. Wilford and Ellen Fair,

> ### The Parker Homestead Logo
>
> One year at the very beginning, Francis Dickson came to visit and look around with her mother, Vivian Sanders. Teressa was talking about needing something to use as a logo, and Francis just sat down in a chair in front of Clark's Cabin with a pencil and paper and quickly sketched a picture of the building, complete with the large tree that once stood in front. And the Parker Homestead logo was born. Francis's hurried drawing is used on every label and publication produced at the Homestead.

who lived across the highway from the Parkers, had an old Home Comfort cookstove. Their stove was bought in 1928 by Mr. Fair's parents and was one of six Home Comfort stoves delivered by train to Harrisburg that year. It was still set up in their kitchen, though it wasn't used as a stove anymore. Mrs. Ellen used it as a countertop. Phil asked to buy the old stove for $100, but Mr. Wilford wouldn't let it go for less than $125. Mrs. Ellen drove a tough bargain herself and insisted that if Phil was going to take her counter, he would have to build her a new one. So he did.

The kitchen addition to Clark's Cabin was completed with the Home Comfort stove, a couple cabinets, a table and chairs and an icebox from Mr. Johnny. Tommye Rosa, Teressa's aunt and our kettle corn lady, relayed a great old-timey kitchen story to me. She said Teressa's great-great-grandmother Nancy Pogue had a special breakfast treat for her children. She would kill an old rooster then dip him in a wash pot full of hot water to help pluck the feathers. She would then cut it up to fry, roll it in flour and cook it in lard over the wood stove. After the chicken was done, she would remove it from the lard pot and place it in a deep iron skillet. Then she covered it with hot water and sprinkled it with flour and put the skillet on the warmer of the wood cookstove for the night. In the morning when they would wake up, the chicken would be so tender that it fell off the bone, and the broth and flour mixture would have turned into gravy. She would then make biscuits, and that's what they would have for breakfast as a special treat. Tommye's grandfather relayed that story to her about his favorite breakfast when he was a child. His mother (the cook) was married in 1908, so the time frame would be pretty close to the time of our Home Comfort stove. (I really liked this story because, to me, it sounds like a 1908 crockpot recipe.)

The Home Comfort in our kitchen really does work—we cooked on it for the Homestead Christmas party for years. I remember Phil's mother, Jean Parker, frying up turkey in there, and it was wonderful. Teressa's aunt Goldie Tedder had a hand in frying the turkey and no one was allowed to sample it while she was cooking. Charlie McClain tried to snitch a piece one year, and Aunt Goldie swatted his hand with the fork, telling him to "get out of that and wait like everybody else." Charlie later remarked that he had not had his hand slapped like that since he was a little boy and his grandma got him.

We have so many great memories of the Homestead's first cabin, and it sat this way in Phil and Teressa's backyard until 2003, when a tornado came through and destroyed the original front part of the house. The Brunson part of the house was saved and is referred to by most as simply "the Kitchen."

Aunt Goldie Tedder, cooking up cracklins. Watch your hand if you try to sneak some! *Parker Family Collection.*

More interesting things around the cabin include a cherry tree that puts off cherries every year. I must admit, they are a little tart for my taste, and I much prefer the pear trees we have out back by the gristmill when it comes time for fruit.

Through the years that Clark's Cabin and the kitchen were at the Homestead, they were used for many things: a hangout, field trip station, place to warm up during the Homestead Holidays events, among others. But for me the most memorable use for Clark's Cabin would have to be as

Clark's Cabin. *Parker Family Collection.*

the best (or worst, depending on how you look at it) station during Haunted Homestead. My husband, Cy, is quite a large and imposing fellow, and once you get his college football pads (XXXL) on him, he is even more so. Cy, I and several of our friends would hang out "up front" around Clark's Cabin and would be the first station at Haunted Homestead.

You see, when you get men of Cy's size and put them in overalls (in the woods in the dark in front of an old log cabin holding machetes and such), it is just a scary thing—a very scary thing. I cannot come close to recalling how many trailer loads of people paid good money and waited in line for hours to go through our haunted house, only to get scared to death in the first two minutes of their tour and turn right around without finishing the next twenty minutes of haunts that lay ahead.

We tried to tell them we were the worst up front and that it would be better past us, but they would have no part of it. Teressa has gotten on to us more than once for being too scary. But you know, we really feel like if you came to be scared, you need to get your money's worth, even if it is only for two minutes. And as a side note, many of our other scarers at stations in the back (including Phil and Teressa) would take their breaks and come up front to Clark's Cabin just to watch us do our thing and scare the fire out of people. We really were that good.

2
THE FIRST FIELD TRIPS

After the dogtrot was complete, Phil and Teressa had themselves an awesome piece of history. Each year, the state of Arkansas has a promotion called Arkansas Heritage Week, and Teressa—by then the Harrisburg Elementary School counselor—went to her principal and asked about bringing the Harrisburg Elementary kids out to see the collection of artifacts.

That first year of Homestead School Kids brought the entire Harrisburg Elementary, kindergarten through fourth grade. The kids loved it. Phil's aunt and uncle Walter and Helen Pilcher dressed up for the kids in period costumes and put on quite a performance. They sat on the porch and pretended to live there, telling stories about the olden days. Aunt Helen churned butter on the porch with a dasher—she would churn all day on that one batch, letting students have a turn at it. And then the showstopper: Uncle Walter and his pocket watch that didn't work. He would proudly display it for all the kids to see, and when they asked him what time it was, he deftly held it to his wrist (and read the time off his wristwatch).

After this momentous first ever Homestead field trip, Teressa was blown away by the kids' reactions, the teacher's positive feedback and her peers' urging for her to do it again. She went and met with the superintendent of Harrisburg Schools at the time, Mr. Jim Parrish, and asked him if he thought there was a larger market out there for the Homestead. Mr. Parrish did not hesitate and encouraged Teressa to give it a try.

After over twenty-five years of field trips, we can definitely say that both Teressa and Mr. Parrish were right. The first year students were scheduled in

Seventeen buses parked for Homestead field trips, circa 2011. *Parker Family Collection.*

Engaged students at a field trip, circa 2010, learning about kettle corn. *Parker Family Collection.*

Outhouse Tips

The first Homestead outhouse, made of reclaimed wood from Teressa's great-grandpa August Heeb's barn. *Parker Family Collection.*

Outhouses during Homestead times were often marked with a sun and a moon on them. Do you know why? Because of widespread illiteracy during the time period, you didn't want people having to try and sort through hieroglyphics to be able to finish their business. The sun stood for masculinity and the moon for femininity, and everyone pretty much had that one figured out when they were quite young. The reason most re-created outhouses have the moon symbol on them and not the sun is because historically men were able to just step back into the woods and do their business, but women needed a private place. In the case that there was only one outhouse, it was generally designated for females. One more fascinating fact: When people would visit an outhouse, they would take two red corncobs with them and one white one. They would use one of the red ones and then use the white one. If the white corncob showed that they needed a little extra attention, they would then use the second red one.

one-hour time slots. A few years later, Harrisburg Elementary was joined by other schools that had heard about Phil and Teressa's log cabin, and as more students came and more buildings went up, the time slots were changed to half days.

The first few years of field trips were so much fun. It was all hands on deck, and anyone that Phil and Teressa could get to come and help was utilized. One year, Phil's aunt Joy Andrews was working in the kitchen. She had not been given the complete rundown on what everything in the cabin was but was not to be deterred—she went for it anyway. When asked about

Corncob Jelly

Teressa has made this jelly using this recipe. It's a great way to use some of those corncobs left after you've put up your corn for the year. This recipe was a blue-ribbon winner at the Northeast Arkansas District Fair.

12 red corncobs, broken into pieces
3 pints of water
1 package of unflavored gelatin, such as Sure-jell
3 cups of sugar
Red food coloring, if desired

Boil broken cobs in the water for 30 minutes. Remove from heat and strain, reserving the water and discarding the cobs. If there's not enough liquid, add water to make 3 cups. Add gelatin and bring to a rolling boil. Add sugar and boil two to three minutes or until the mixture reaches jelly stage. The test for jelly stage is simple. First, remove jelly from heat. Have two or three small plates chilling in the freezer. Place 1 teaspoon of hot jelly or jam on plate and freeze for 1 minute. Remove from freezer. Surface should wrinkle when edge is pushed with finger. If surface doesn't wrinkle, continue cooking and repeat test every few minutes. Once your jelly has reached jelly stage, add food coloring (if desired) and pour into hot jars and seal. If you can't find red corncobs, you can use regular ones.

---

a tumbling butter churn, she on the spot said it was an old washing machine. Aunt Joy went into great detail about how you loaded the clothes and spun it to wash. That was one hardworking butter churn. And the bad part was that none of the teachers or students knew the difference.

One year, a friend of mine from college, Travis Eddleman, worked the Homestead field trips as the storyteller. He played a funny, likeable, all-around scoundrel kind of character. While visiting with Cy on his lunch break, Travis said he was thinking about "stealing a ham" from the general store as a skit. What Travis didn't plan on was the fact that when he stole the ham an eager herd of schoolchildren, armed with walking sticks they had purchased from the store, would chase him down. They

> ## Teressa's Buttermilk Pie
>
> A favorite at the Homestead has always been homemade butter. Teressa's sister Alyce Gustafson was the first real butter maker at the Homestead. At the time, Alyce was able to buy five-gallon buckets of cream from a dairy. She used a butter churn with a dasher and a tumbling churn for larger amounts. She got really adept at using butter paddles to work all the milk out of the butter and sold everything she could make, often running out before the day was over. Today, the Women's Civilian Corps of the Seventh Arkansas Civil War Reenactors have taken over. Even now—twenty plus years later—they are never able to make enough butter for demand.
>
> *3 eggs*
> *1 cup buttermilk*
> *1 stick butter, softened*
> *1½ cups sugar*
> *3 tablespoons flour*
> *1 teaspoon vanilla*
> *Dash nutmeg*
> *Premade or store-bought pie shell*
>
> Combine all ingredients, in order, except the pie shell. Blend together until well mixed. Pour into unbaked pie shell and bake for 45 to 50 minutes at 350 degrees.

poked at him with their sticks until he gave them the ham back. The vigilantes promptly returned the ham, which was really a sack stuffed with newspaper to look like a ham, to the store. They all kept their eye on Travis the rest of the day.

Homestead School Kids has grown quite a bit since Uncle Walter and Aunt Helen sat on the porch. In recent years, it is an all-day event, hosting one thousand plus children on our busiest days and with four and six thousand students attending our field trips each year. Stations have included broom making, sorghum cooking, butter churning, grist milling, kettle corn making, lye soap washing, quilting, beekeeping, archeology, farm animals, newspaper printing, animal furs, rope making, gospel and bluegrass musicians, itinerant preaching, crosscut sawing, blacksmithing, turn-of-the-century farming, storytelling, herb gardening, one-room school education, wool spinning and much more.

Perhaps the most satisfying aspect of our field trips is that each of the past few years, we have spoken with parents attending our field trips with their children who say that they themselves attended as a child. The parents are always amazed at how much the Homestead has grown and are excited to share their childhood experiences with their own children.

The field trips are the most tiring thing we do here at Homestead, but they are also the most worthwhile. There is nothing quite like seeing a child take his or her first taste of sorghum molasses—his or her face either spreads with a big smile or contorts with a look of agony, and we would have it no other way. Either reaction is a great lesson about what our forefathers had to use, good or bad, just to get by and to have something sweet.

Homestead will go from a handful of workers (and by "workers" I mean Phil, Teressa, Cy and me) to upward of fifty to put on the field trips. Many, like J.C. Smith, have been every year. Genny Sadler is one of my favorite field-trip workers to see coming, as she is always checking to see if Cy and I have something to drink or need any lunch. It is wonderful to have her think about and take care of us because when you see a thousand people in groups of twenty-five or so in a four-hour period, there is not much time to leave the porch.

3

PHIL

His Great Sorghum Adventure and the First Festival

It appeared that Phil's little hangout was beginning to get out of hand. Not only did Phil have Teressa bringing the entire Harrisburg Elementary to see it, but he also kept thinking about things that would add to it, go with it or might just be cool to have. And this led him to thinking about sorghum—a lot. And according to Teressa, he talked about it even more.

He just about drove her crazy going on and on for a couple years about how they should grow and cook sorghum before she finally gave in and told him that her great-uncle Howard Tedder had a sorghum mill. Teressa remembered seeing him cook sorghum on it when she was a child. Phil couldn't believe it, so they headed for Uncle Howard's right away.

Uncle Howard met them, loaded them into his pickup truck and then drove them deep into the woods. Teressa laughed telling me about it—she motioned like she was chopping at vines and sticker bushes with a hoe, and I guess that's what Uncle Howard was doing. She said he would holler, "There's a piece! Oh here's some more…" and then would bend down and study it before declaring, "Yep, it's all there."

So Phil had himself a mill. And that year Phil's daddy, Robert (Bob) Parker, bought a copper sorghum pan from Leland Carter and gave it to Phil for Christmas. Now that Phil had what you might call an entire sorghum factory, he just needed some cane.

But the next problem was that Phil didn't have anywhere to grow sorghum. Enlisting the help of a good friend, Charlie McClain (who had a place around Heber Springs), Phil was finally able to plant some sorghum,

Phil Parker smiling in front of his sorghum pan, circa 2010. *Parker Family Collection*.

A batch of sorghum cooking at the Homestead. *Parker Family Collection.*

and the next fall, Phil and Charlie hauled back a truckload of cane. They thought they were really going have something. Phil had told a few people in town—mostly friends and family—that they were going to squeeze and cook sorghum on Saturday. Two hundred people showed up.

That first batch was a real ramshackle operation. The sorghum mill Phil and Teressa had was a mule-driven mill, which meant you tied up a mule to the mill and made it go in circles, turning the mill and squeezing the juice out of the cane. Well, they didn't have a mule, but Phil and Teressa didn't let something like that get them down. They called up Phil's cousin Billy Wayne Pilcher, and he brought over his donkey named Amos. They squeezed their truckload of cane and thought they really had a lot of juice. Phil, Charlie and some others in attendance set the copper pan up on blocks and built a fire under it. They got ready to cook for the crowd while Teressa went back and forth to her kitchen to cook a bunch of biscuits for all the company to eat the sorghum with.

Another thing that was funny about that day was that out of the attending crowd, many, many people professed to knowing all about how to cook sorghum. The problem was that they all knew how to do it differently. There were many instructions, helpful hints and out-and-out suggestions that were thrown around at the first cooking, but everyone was having a great time.

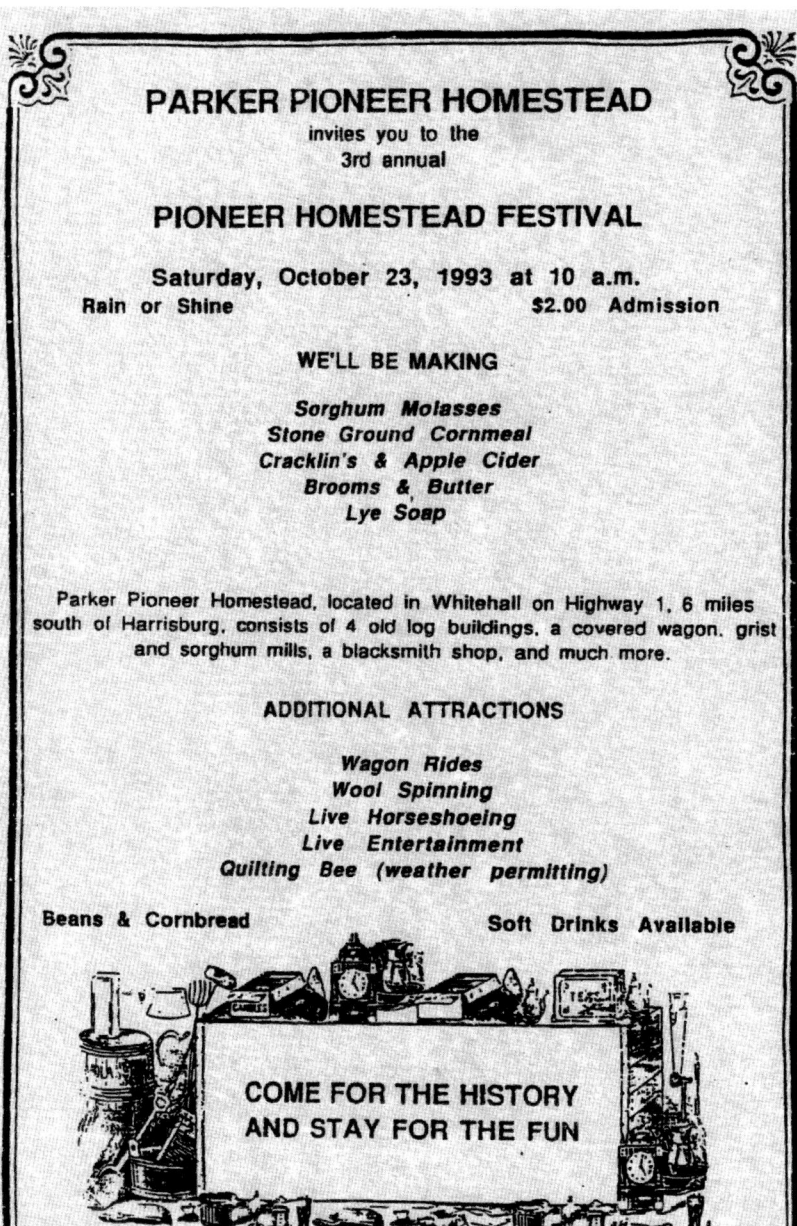

A promotional flyer from the third-annual Homestead Festival. *Parker Family Collection.*

One thing that Phil and Teressa did not know was that when you cook the juice down to make the sorghum a lot of it boils out and evaporates. As a matter of fact, most of it does. For every six to twelve gallons of juice you have, you will get about one gallon of syrup. When I interviewed Phil and Teressa about that day, Phil said he thought they made about three, maybe four, gallons of sorghum. Teressa laughed and said she didn't think it was anywhere near that much. She remembered a picture of that first batch showing a few jars sitting on a board on the ground. She thought it was maybe five or six jars in varying sizes—whatever they had around. But the one thing they both agreed on about that day is that with two hundred people there to eat the finished product, they didn't have any left.

Phil and Teressa refer to that day as the first Homestead Festival, an annual event based around sorghum cooking that has grown each year. Originally, the Homestead Festival consisted of only one day: the third Saturday in October. This day was picked because the first weekend wouldn't work—it was too close to the end of field trips. The second weekend was out because the Weiner Rice Festival was held then, and it is only twenty or so miles away from the Homestead. The fourth weekend was the big festival in Corning, and in later years, that weekend would conflict with Haunted Homestead. So the third Saturday it was.

After a few years of festival, it became evident that a one-day event with a handful of family members to run it was not going to be enough, so Sunday afternoon was added. It was a little slow on that first Sunday, and Phil and Teressa worried that their expansion plan would not work. But around 1:30 p.m., people started coming in, and the first full weekend of festival was a success. I remember the first festival I attended. It was in 2000, and we were parking cars at Mr. Johnny Roberts's house (where I now live) and hauling people down the road from there to the Homestead on sixteen-foot trailers, almost like a hay ride. I remember a few years after that, a couple of Cy's cousins, Brody Heeb and Matt Parker, pulled the trailers in a continuous circle all day long. They were high schoolers and would get out and help ladies on and off the trailer, and then they would tip their hats before getting back in and making another round.

Another funny story from the early years is the time Teressa gave her sister Alyce a check for $325 to cash at the bank to use for change at the festival. When Alyce got to the bank, there was not enough in Phil and Teressa's account to cover the check, so Alyce wrote her own check to get the change for festival. Talk about saving the day. Of course, once the festival was done, Alyce was paid back in full. Today, $325 would not even begin to cover the amount of change needed for the one-weekend event.

Several years back, there was a huge rainstorm that lasted almost all festival weekend. It was enough that Phil and Teressa were forced to close the gate. The mule had gone home, and no one was coming. The Parkers were not able to "pay out" that year and had to go borrow the money to clear up debts incurred to put on the festival. After that awful experience, Phil and Teressa began looking at adding another weekend, in case of rain. They ended up deciding on the second weekend in October, the Rice Festival weekend, and thought that maybe local people would go and support both events since the two festivals were held in such proximity. And local people did just that—there have even been years that the second weekend was bigger than the original third weekend date.

Of course the main draw for the festival is sorghum. Sorghum has been planted and harvested in all kinds of places since that first crop in Heber—at Robert Parker's house across the highway in Whitehall; at Jimmy Heeb's (Teressa's daddy) farm west of Harrisburg; and now at the Homestead.

Our cooking area has changed a little bit, too. The sorghum shed sits next to the post office and has three separate stations. The first is where visitors can watch the mule-driven mill squeeze the cane while a worker feeds in a stalk or two at a time. Watching the green juice pour out is kind of a shock for many people who are familiar with the dark caramel color of the finished

> ## Tales from Teressa
>
> *I was entering the national sorghum cooking contest at the annual convention for the National Sweet Sorghum Producers and Processors Association in Pigeon Forge, Tennessee, for the first time. Mail outs indicated that there were kitchens available in certain rooms for ease of cooking your entry. I gathered all the supplies needed and headed that way. Once we arrived, I discovered that the "kitchen" was a kitchenette with no oven to bake the bread pudding in. I talked to the front desk, but they offered no help. I couldn't use the hotel's restaurant oven because of health regulations. I even tried the local senior citizen center—it wasn't available. So I started calling around to churches until I found one willing to let me use its kitchen. The secretary's husband met me there early the morning of the contest and talked me into using the convection oven, which I had never done before. I made a double batch, and it was not fully cooked, although it looked like it. Still ended up with a red ribbon for second place, but I really think it would have been a blue if I had used a regular oven.*

Our sweet sorghum ladies: (left to right) Vivian Sanders, Clara Tarkington, Berneda Heeb, Estelle Jones and Sylvia Condra. *Parker Family Collection.*

product, but they can step over to the cooking station and watch that process before their eyes.

Green juice is poured into the now stainless-steel pan by the sorghum cookers. It is boiled down as it makes its way through the pan, which is situated like a maze. The cookers can open and close sections of the pan as they need to, ensuring that the sorghum on the end is the right color, texture and consistency. When the green juice makes it all the way to the end of the pan, it is poured into a stainless-steel tank to be bottled up in jars. When you're walking by, notice the brick sculpture of a sorghum stalk behind the cookers—Phil made that!

Station three is where sorghum lovers as well as curious first-time tasters can line up to try a bit. The sorghum tastin' area was manned for years by the Poinsett County Extension Homemakers Club. Teressa said that most of the ladies were in their eighties and had been running a booth at the Poinsett County fair every year. It was getting to be a lot of work for them to set up and over dinner at Teressa's grandma Berneda's house one Sunday, she told them she would help out. Teressa made all of their displays for them, and in exchange, they volunteered to be the sorghum ladies.

Bread Pudding with Sorghum Sauce

Bread Pudding

½ cup brown sugar
½ cup white sugar
2 eggs
2 cups milk
¼ cup butter, melted
Assorted deli croissants, torn into pieces.

Mix together brown sugar, white sugar, eggs, milk and butter. Add torn croissants and toss to combine. Pour into a baking dish and bake at 400 degrees for 45 minutes. When done, top with Sorghum Sauce (recipe below).

Sorghum Sauce

½ cup light brown sugar
1 tablespoon sorghum
1 tablespoon light corn syrup, such as Karo
¼ cup butter
½ cup heavy cream
1½ teaspoons vanilla

Combine all ingredients in saucepan over medium heat. Bring to a boil, stirring frequently. Reduce to medium low and boil for 5 minutes. Remove from heat. Sauce will thicken as it cools.

The sorghum ladies are a real staple at the Homestead, and though many of them have since passed away, we are so thankful to have had them as part of our lives and as part of Homestead history. Berneda Heeb, Vivian Sanders, Sylvia Condra and Estelle Jones were the main sorghum ladies, but they were joined by other friends, such as Margaret Mann, Clara Tarkington, Ruthie Roberts, Jimmie McGee and more. The sorghum mill's beginning-to-end process is one that visitors are fascinated by festival after festival.

When the sorghum cooking was just getting started, Phil and Teressa really needed someone who could bring out a mule to run the mill. LaFarrell Wess, who was, at that time, Phil and Teressa's mailman, said that he knew somebody—Wilburn Swanner. He brought him out, and Wilburn took a look around. Finally, he said, "I'll do it," and he showed up to run the sorghum mill every year until he died.

Mr. Swanner had some pretty good stories from his youth, such as being arrested for hauling a wagon full of sugar. He was accused of being a moonshiner by the "Regulators," or Prohibition agents, and locked up in jail. While Mr. Swanner sat in jail, the Regulators arrested another alleged moonshiner who talked them into taking him home to change clothes before taking him

Left: Cy Parker in his great-grandpa Dode Heeb's wagon. *Parker Family Collection.*

Below: Sweet Sorghum sign above the Sorghum ladies' stand. *Parker Family Collection.*

to jail. He went inside and then came back out shooting, killing the two officers. Without the officers' sworn statements, Mr. Swanner was free to go. Though the Homestead may or may not have had an expert moonshiner, we never have invested in a still on our grounds.

When Wilburn got sick, he told Phil that he thought he had hoed his last row. Phil remembers telling him that it was a good long row, and Wilburn agreed. Wilburn's friend Chuck Webb had been helping him every year out at the sorghum mill, and he took Phil aside and said, "Don't you worry about sorghum, I'll take care of it." And take care of it he did. Papa Chuck and James Holmes ran the operation with horses and a mule named John Henry. John Henry was originally owned by James but was sold to Chuck, and after some time, Chuck sold him back to James. No matter his ownership, John Henry worked the Homestead every year.

When the Homestead inherited "Papa Chuck," we got his whole family. Chuck's brother Carl is one of our main sorghum men and has been a staple at Homestead events since the beginning. Chuck's wife, Wanda, now heads up our sorghum ladies. At any given festival, if you have taken a wagon ride, had your car parked, tasted some sorghum or bought anything in the store, you have had an interaction with Papa Chuck and his family.

We have even built a little area behind our house that we affectionately call "the gypsy camp." It is the area where Chuck and his family camp out each festival. Many a night, there will be twenty or more people around the fire—including me and my kids—eating, laughing and enjoying one another's company. Though Papa Chuck has now passed away, we are so thankful to have known him and are also thankful for his wonderful family, who we gladly claim as our own.

Bob Parker—or Granddad, as everyone called him—was our main sorghum cook for years until he passed away in 2004, when Phil took over the operation. Phil and his friend Mark Sadler are currently our main cooks at School Kids and the festival, but there is a huge crew that comes out each Labor Day weekend for the annual first sorghum cook, including Mark's wife, Genny, who is an expert cook in her own right.

A funny story about Phil and Mark is from several years back. After cooking a batch of sorghum they were particularly proud of, they decided to enter it in the Northeast Arkansas District Fair. They entered two bottles from the same batch—one with Phil's name as cook and one with Mark's. Well, someone had to be named winner. Suffice it to say that even though Parker Homestead is the proud owner of the first- and second-place ribbons from the fair that year, Mark was the first-place cook.

> ### Pecan Pie Muffins
>
> Mrs. Sylvia Condra, an original Homestead sorghum lady and town legend, used to make Cy pecan pies every year. They have always been his favorite. Though I have tried and tried several recipes and fancy myself to be a very decent cook, I cannot make anything resembling a "Mrs. Sylvia Pie." So when Cy's aunt Alyce made these pecan pie muffins, and I watched Cy devour them, I had to have the recipe. It is easy and wonderful, and you will love them.
>
> 1 cup light brown sugar, packed
> ½ cup flour
> 2 eggs, beaten
> ⅔ cup butter, softened
> 1 cup chopped pecans
>
> In a medium bowl, mix together dry ingredients. Add beaten eggs, butter and pecans and stir until blended. Spoon batter into muffin cups (or a greased muffin pan) and bake at 350 for 20 to 25 minutes.

Though sorghum is our main draw to the Homestead, the Parkers are kind of hit and miss when it comes to inheriting the "we love to eat sorghum" gene. Cy, Caroline and I don't appreciate it like we should, though Kaiser would drink it out of the bottle if we would let him. Phil and Teressa's granddaughter Kyra Burns also loves it, as does Phil. Teressa doesn't care for it much but does cook with it and makes some awesome sorghum bread pudding.

My papaw Louis Childers never did like sorghum. He said his daddy, Andrew Childers, raised a little bit when he was a kid, but Andrew would also squeeze and cook for others who raised it. Instead of his father being paid wages for his sorghum work, he was paid with a percentage of the finished batch. Needless to say, Papaw ate a little too much sorghum as a child and got burned out on it pretty young.

Now, Papaw was one of eleven children, and times were hard during the 1920s and '30s. He said that they would only get one pair of shoes a year, usually in the fall to hopefully get them through the winter. One year—he thought it was in the late 1920s—he and his older brothers were bringing a wagon full of sorghum back to the house when the mule got spooked and jumped. The wagon lurched, and a big container of sorghum spilled all over Papaw and his new shoes, ruining them. He said even his brothers felt sorry for him, and that was really saying something.

But don't let us tell you about sorghum, you really should try for yourself. The principal sweetenin' of pioneers is still wildly popular for a reason and can't be all bad. Just ask Kyra and Kaiser.

Bob "Granddad" Parker

After the first sorghum cooking, Granddad (Bob Parker) became enthused about the whole enterprise. In fact, he was not only enthused but also sort of took over the whole sorghum operation. He went on the hunt for equipment and bought the first Homestead Farmall tractor from "a little old lady" for $125. It was completely frozen up, and the common consensus was that it would never run. But Granddad was from the old school and worked nonstop for days on the old tractor until he got it running. The first time he drove it, he ran it up and down Parker Road cutting doughnuts.

Armed with a tractor, he now needed planting equipment and some ground to farm. He bought a small plot of land right behind his home from Carl Woodham and procured some sorghum seed from Leo "Pete" Rolland of Cherry Valley. After he had his own crop, Granddad started saving his seed from year to year, keeping it stored in his freezer. Early each year, he would take out a few seeds and place them in a damp paper towel to see if they would sprout, just to make sure his seeds were still good. During this time, Granddad also got a gee whiz, or a horse-drawn plow, and a cultivator from Kenneth Brand. He bought an old two-row planter from Randy Jones of Harrisburg, and all of a sudden, Granddad was in business.

He set up a sorghum mill that Phil had bought from the King family in Paragould in his backyard. It was a Chattanooga Plow belt-driven mill, which saved time because it would take handfuls of stalks at a time instead of just one or two, and he didn't need to use mules to power it. Even with the technological advances in the mill, Granddad still had to strip all the leaves off the sorghum by hand and then cut the stalks down with a machete. It would take him days to get all of it, and then, he would let it lay in the field for three to five days before he would start cooking. To gather the cane, he had his father, Henry (or Papa) Parker, drive the truck through the field, pulling a trailer for Granddad and Phil to hand load the cane on.

On the first few go-rounds, Granddad would squeeze the cane one day and then ice the fifty-gallon barrels of juice down to try to keep it from spoiling overnight. But that didn't work. Papa showed up at Phil's house for

Bob "Granddad" Parker cooking sorghum, circa 1990s. *Parker Family Collection.*

the cooking and said, "Son, your juice is soured; it's ruint, it ain't no good!" Well, Granddad didn't like to hear that, and the pan was emptied and waited for another day.

The process made a change after that. Granddad would start stacking the cut cane up at the mill, and then on weekends he wanted to cook, he and Phil would get up early and start squeezing cane, about 4:30 a.m. Mark Sadler and Carl Steyer usually showed up to help, too. Granddad was now the self-proclaimed head cooker, so Phil and Carl took care of the fire under the pan while Mark helped Granddad cook. Some days it worked, and some days it didn't, as everyone involved was still learning about sorghum. Pete Rolland was always there to lend a hand if he could, as he had his own crop of sorghum.

With Granddad as the head sorghum cooker, Phil was able to work on more buildings during the weekends. Granddad would work the field during the week while Phil was at work, and on the weekends, he would help Phil and Cy build. One summer while Phil was at work, Teressa and Granddad put in the brick floor under the sorghum shed. It sounds crazy, but during that time, it was literally all hands on deck and never a dull or wasted moment.

In the meantime, Phil was gathering up more sorghum mills to place along the fence row or to use as exhibits. Years later, Teressa remembered sitting through a presentation about sorghum mills at the National Sorghum Convention, and for just about every picture that was shown, Phil would lean over and say, "We have one of those" or "That one is down at Daddy's" and "There's one of those at the green pole barn," which prompted Teressa to ask, "Just how many mills do you have?"

It turned out he had quite a few, and she wasn't even aware of it. This revelation shouldn't have come as much of a surprise, though, because by then, their whole lives revolved around Homestead. One year, Phil bought Teressa not one, but two hit-and-miss motors for her birthday, and another year she received a Farmall B tractor, and so on and so forth.

Things went along this way for several years, until the summer of 2004. Granddad was beginning to lose interest in things and just didn't feel well. Phil's mother, Jean, drove Granddad over to see the new brush arbor, and he didn't want to get out of the car. He said it looked nice and then added, "Now, take me back home." Granddad had been the driving force behind Homestead and left his mark everywhere. He was the groundskeeper, watchdog, straw boss, problem solver, farmer and so much more. He passed away two weeks before the scheduled field trips for that year, and with thousands of kids scheduled, the show had to go on.

Phil took over sorghum, though he only knew the basics from what he had observed Granddad do. County extension agent Rick Thompson had worked side by side with Granddad at the sorghum pan for years, and he was there to help Phil, though he always said, "Nobody can cook sorghum like Mr. Parker." With Phil moving up to sorghum, Cy moved up to brooms, and the Homestead moved on.

Though things have been running this way for going on ten years now, there is no doubt that Granddad's heart and soul can still be seen all over the Homestead. We miss him greatly, but out at the place, we feel like he is still right there with us.

4

THE AFTERMATH OF THE FIRST SORGHUM COOKIN'

Strange things started happening after that first sorghum cookin'. Phil and Teressa would come home from work and find old, rusty things in their driveway that had been donated. Their answering machine would be full of messages with people wanting to donate or telling about a cabin they knew about. Before the cookin', it was almost like everyone was holding their breath to see whether or not the Homestead would turn into anything. Well after the cooking, it seemed everyone decided that it had, and the full force of the community was thrown behind Phil and Teressa. Over the next few years, Whitehall residents began to donate things to Phil and Teressa like mad. They had inadvertently become the keepers of the community's memories, the collectors of Whitehall's past. Teressa once remarked that it seemed like all of the artifacts were finding their way back home.

Items received during this time are too numerous to recount here, but I will name a few of note: the old Whitehall gristmill, the old hand scales out of the Whitehall gin, school desks out of the Whitehall school, a Number 4 Sears and Roebuck school bell, a cigar case, a McCaskey filing system, a coffee grinder, and the list goes on and on.

Phil and Teressa also had many adventures during this time period. One day, Mr. Travis Vaughn of Hydrick showed up and relayed to Phil that there was a large cabin in good shape with great big, wide logs. Teressa motioned and held her hand apart about eighteen inches or so when telling me about the description of the logs. Mr. Vaughn said he'd just been by it in the last year or so. Of course, Phil was excited, and he and Mr. Vaughn

Sorghum Cream Pie
Blue-ribbon Winner at the National Sorghum Convention 2013

The Homestead sorghum pan and cooking area, early 2000s. *Parker Family Collection.*

¾ cup white sugar
¼ cup sorghum
2 cups half-and-half
⅛ teaspoon salt
½ cup heavy whipping cream
¼ cup brown sugar
¼ cup cornstarch
½ cup (1 stick) butter
1 teaspoon vanilla
1 premade or store-bought unbaked pie shell
Pinch cinnamon
Pinch nutmeg

In a saucepan, bring to a boil white sugar, sorghum, half-and-half, salt and whipping cream. In another saucepan, combine brown sugar and cornstarch. Whisk hot mixture into brown sugar mixture. Add butter and cook over medium heat for 5 minutes or until thick, whisking constantly. Simmer 1 minute and stir in vanilla. Pour into unbaked pie shell and sprinkle with cinnamon and nutmeg. Bake at 375 degrees for 25 minutes.

Kaiser Parker standing in front of the sorghum crop. *Parker Family Collection.*

loaded up to drive to the location and see the cabin. They drove around a bit looking, and when they got there, the cabin was in complete ruin, rotten beyond repair. Mr. Vaughn scratched his head and said, "I guess it's been a little longer than I thought since I've been up here."

Phil was still able to salvage two logs from the cabin, and they were made into benches. They now sit on the porch of the schoolhouse.

Other items that made their way to the Homestead in the following years included a peanut thresher, on lifetime loan from the Arkansas State University Museum; the old blackboard from the Weiner Catholic School; and even bridge timbers out of the Poinsett County landfill. One of the more interesting items donated is a log from Claypool's reservoir. It had been chewed and cut down by beavers and was donated by Lanny Riley to be used on field trips for a science example.

Teressa gathered up family, community and historic recipes and put out the Homestead cookbook, and also around this time, she began making lye soap. Many things were coming together, though Phil and Teressa still did not have any type of concrete plan about what they would build or do next

> ## Sorghum Hot Chocolate
> *Blue-ribbon Winner at the National Sorghum Convention 2013*
>
> 1 cup sugar
> ¼ cup sorghum
> 2 cups half-and-half
> 1 cup heavy cream
> ⅛ cup cocoa
> 3 cups milk
>
> Mix everything except milk in saucepan and bring to a boil. Stir in milk and serve piping hot.

or really any idea about where the Homestead was going. They just took what they were given, bought what they could afford and went from there.

As the Homestead grew, they began running out of space—quickly. Their backyard could hold only so many cabins. Phil and Teressa had planted a row of pine trees in front of the little barn because they never had any intention of the Homestead growing any farther back. The owner of the property behind theirs, which was mostly wooded, was John McDermott. Phil went to him to try to buy an acre or two. He wouldn't sell but told Phil he could go ahead and build some on it because he wasn't using the land and also because he liked what Phil and Teressa were doing.

When Mr. McDermott sold his farm to Billy Denton of Wilson, Arkansas, Phil was scared to death. They had already built some on Mr. Denton's land and were getting ready to build the general store. Phil went to Billy and asked about buying a few acres, and Billy also turned him down but said it would be OK for Phil and Teressa to continue on with Mr. McDermott's agreement.

To those of you who are familiar with the Homestead, all of the land from behind Clark's Cabin back toward the covered bridge was owned by Billy. Phil and Teressa had not built much on it, but things were really about to expand exponentially. Phil asked Billy one more time about purchasing some land, and instead of selling any land, Billy gave Phil permission to build the big barn. Some years later, Billy decided to fence in his property with a ten-foot fence, and he came over and told Phil what he was planning to do. Billy asked Phil how much ground he wanted before he put the fence up, and Phil replied he would like to buy over to the pine-tree border and up to the big oak tree that sits on the backside of what was Mr. Johnny and Mrs. Ruthie's property. All in all, Billy sold Phil and Teressa about thirty acres of ground, and the new addition was immediately utilized, becoming the parking lot, a new entrance and some farm ground to finally raise the sorghum crop on the grounds.

We were wonderfully fortunate to have great neighbors. And speaking of neighbors, it was Mr. John E. Roberts, one of Phil and Teressa's neighbors, who was walking around the place looking at things when he commented, "The Parkers have a real pioneer homestead." And thus Parker Homestead was named. Again and again, I hope one thing that is conveyed in this book is that the Homestead was built cabin by cabin by a community of so many, and for them we are so grateful.

The National Sweet Sorghum Producers and Processers Association

Though Phil had been aware of the existence of a sorghum association for some time, Granddad was never the least bit interested in finding out more about it. Once Granddad passed away, Phil was very interested because he needed help. Help with all aspects of sorghum, but mostly, he needed help with how to make it less labor intensive.

Joining the association, Phil learned about cutting cane with a corn binder, which cuts several stalks at a time and binds them together, making it possible to pick up several stalks at a time. Our neighbor Mr. Bob Young will pull the truck while Phil, Cy, Mark and Carl load the cane. We now have a head cutter, built by Carl and his brother Martin, and are still looking for more innovations. Phil has completed a new sorghum house, which has been approved by the health department, enabling him to sell sorghum at outlets other than the Homestead. He plans to start cooking over gas, another thing he learned from the sorghum association, but Homestead will always use Uncle Howard's mule-drawn sorghum mill and cook over wood for show.

5

THE THREE PARKER HOMESTEAD BARNS

Phil went and bought a little barn from Charlie Worley. It was located south of Whitehall on the ridge past Clampitt Cemetery. The small one-room cabin was used as a corncrib, and Phil paid ten dollars for it. Best estimates are that it was built sometime in the 1880s, and the type of notching on the logs is called chamfer and notch—it is of German origin and tells us a little about the builder.

Phil stocked his new barn with things like saw blades and old tools, and he did his best to make it look like an old working barn. When they first got it, Phil remembered thinking they would never have enough stuff to fill it up. Just a few short years later, it became apparent that the Homestead needed a much bigger barn, and the original barn became known as "the little barn."

Now, around the time that Phil began thinking the little barn was a wee bit too small, he heard that Square Deal, a Harrisburg businessman, had dismantled and brought home the logs from the old American Legion Hut in Trumann, Arkansas. It was built by the Civilian Conservation Corps in the 1930s and was very large. Phil wondered if maybe he could buy enough logs from Square Deal to build a new, larger barn and then set off to ask as much.

At Square Deal's, Phil asked him how much it would be to buy just a few of the logs. Square Deal looked at the enormous pile and thought for a minute. Finally, he offered up, "One dollar a foot." Phil thought quietly for a minute then asked "How much for all of them?" Square Deal paused then said, "Two hundred dollars."

Sold.

The little barn. *Parker Family Collection.*

There were enough American Legion Logs to build the new barn much larger than Phil was planning on. It ended up measuring thirty by fifty feet. The tin for the roof came off an old equipment shed from Jimmy Winningham's farm. Phil even had enough logs left over for two additional buildings, the blacksmith shop and the way station. The two-hundred-dollar deal was perhaps the best deal on logs Phil ever got.

During School Kids, our local county extension agents will set up shop in the big barn and teach students about farm equipment and Depression-era agricultural practices and will also show off the Homestead donkey Julie Bell. Phil and Teressa's vision for the barn was to make it look like someone had just walked off from working there—you will see crosscut saws, old hit-and-miss engines and the old cotton scales from the Whitehall gin. Take your time and look around—no telling what kinds of treasures you may find.

Be sure to notice the plantation bell set just outside the barn to the southwest. It was donated by Mr. Ed Hollan of Wynne and came off his grandpa's plantation in Mississippi. The plantation measured two miles across and the bell sat in the middle. It was used to call in the hands and could easily be heard a mile away. Also set by the bell is the crosscut saw

A History and Guide

The Homestead barn one winter in the early 2000s. *Parker Family Collection.*

area, one of which came out of the Halk store in Cherry Valley. Though it was most likely fifty years old or better, when we got it, the saw was still "brand new" and wrapped in paper.

You might not think it, but the barn is a very popular place for parties and weddings. Cy and I got married in front of it in 2003. About our wedding, Cy told me he didn't care what I wanted him to wear, or eat or how many pictures I would put him through, and in exchange for all of that, he only had one request. And that was that we would get married in front of the barn he built himself, and I decided that was a very small price to pay in exchange for wedding pictures with no complaining.

Since our wedding, there have been many others staged there; some have been prominently featured in magazine articles and websites. It is a beautiful location, and I think it's good luck as well.

You would think with all the wonderful things the big barn is that Phil would have stopped building barns. But as the Homestead continued to grow (and Phil and Teressa continued to acquire more and more antiques and treasures), the need for additional storage place was becoming a real, pressing issue. Cy spoke to some people with the local utility company, and they agreed to donate several old utility poles for the Homestead to construct a pole barn with. Now this is where a small family disagreement ensued.

Quilting

For years, Phil's mother, Jean, set up and demonstrated quilting for our School Kids event. Jean served as director of the Crowley's Ridge quilt shop in Jonesboro for several years and even had her business making quilts for a store in Seattle, Washington. All families in rural Poinsett County sewed their own clothes, made their own quilts and darned their own socks. Sewing, knitting and crocheting were necessary skills. When times were especially tough, families would not be able to buy nice new fabric for new dresses and trousers, so they would use feed sacks if they had to. Many of the businesses selling feed caught on to this trend and starting making their sacks come in pretty prints to encourage people to pick their brand over another brand of feed in a plainer sack. Feed sack quilts are some of the most prized and sought-after collectible items from the homestead time period.

Cy wanted to build the pole barn forty by two hundred feet. Phil wanted to build it thirty by fifty feet. Somewhere along the way a compromise was made, and it was originally constructed at a size of thirty by one hundred feet. Cy and a couple of his college friends—Steve Marsh, Roger Leder and Nick Martinez—tore tin off old chicken houses in the Conway area to roof the pole barn with. Though Cy was unhappy with the size, Phil thought the pole barn looked great.

And then, they got word about the largest sorghum mill in America being up for sale.

At one time, Vaughn Wilson was the largest sorghum producer in the United States, and his mill was legendary in the sorghum world. After Mr. Wilson's death, Phil had contacted his family a couple times before about buying it, but they never were interested in letting it go. Once, he was told that they would not sell just the mill alone—it would have to go with their whole operation at a price of $1 million.

A few years later, Cy was working in Batesville (his first job out of college) and ran into Jesse Kelley of Sulphur Rock. Cy and Jesse got to talking, and before too long, Jesse told Cy he used to work on a sorghum farm for Vaughn Wilson. That got Cy thinking about the mill again, and he asked Phil what he would be willing to pay for it.

Phil said, "We can't afford it."

Cy said, "Maybe, but how much would you pay?"

Cream Puff

Cream Puff is the Homestead's old bob truck, which Phil bought just for sorghum production, specifically for hauling the plummies. It gets its name for its particularly rusty appearance. When the sorghum stalks are squeezed, they make their way out of the mill and up a conveyor until they are dumped into Cream Puff. The kids love to sit in the back of the truck and get covered in plummies.

Kyra and Kaiser in the back of Cream Puff with the plummies. *Parker Family Collection.*

Phil bought Cream Puff for $500 a few years back. When Cy and I took him to go pick it up, it was raining, and Cream Puff's windshield wipers don't work. Oh, and the latch on the driver's side door is busted too. So we followed Phil home with his arm out the window to hold the door closed and his head out the window to see his way home in the rain. Cy and I laughed the whole way, and that twelve-mile drive behind Phil in Cream Puff was one of the most enjoyable of any I ever remember taking.

Phil said, "You'll never get them to sell it."

Cy said, "Maybe, but Dad give me a price."

Phil said, "I guess $2,500."

So Cy called the family of Mr. Vaughn Wilson, who lived in Bethesda, and asked about buying the mill. Situations oftentimes change, and the family realized that the largest sorghum mill in America was not doing anyone any good sitting in a shed not being used. So low and behold, when Cy offered $2,500, they took it.

The mill is very unique to sorghum production. It is a five-roller sugar cane mill that was cast in a foundry in Alexandria, Louisiana, in the late 1800s. When in operation for Mr. Wilson, the mill ran constantly, 24/7, and squeezed between sixteen and twenty-four thousand gallons of sorghum

Sorghum workers, (left to right) Phil, Carl Steyer, Cy, Kyra and Mark Sadler resting on an unloaded sorghum trailer, Farmall tractor and the corn binder visible in background, *Parker Family Collection*.

juice through every day. Mr. Wilson cooked around two thousand gallons of sorghum syrup every day until he ran out of crop, and he planted four hundred acres of cane.

Another thing unique to Mr. Wilson's operation was his use of plummies. Plummies are the sorghum stalks that have already been squeezed of their juice. At Parker Homestead, we feed some to our animals (Julie Bell loves them). But Mr. Wilson burned his plummies to run a huge boiler, and the steam from the boiler is what cooked his juice into syrup.

Phil, Teressa, Cy, Caroline, Mark Sadler, Carl Steyer and I set off to get the mill, and Charlie and Linda McClain drove from Heber Springs to meet us there. It took several trips and a lot of elbow grease to get it dismantled and to the Homestead. They were scary trips there and back, pulling trailers loaded with SkyTracks, but somehow we made it.

Though our operation is nowhere near the scale of Mr. Wilson's, his mill revolutionized our sorghum production at the Homestead. In the days before the mill, when using our hand-fed or mule-driven mills, Phil and

The Tractor Displays

Another attraction at our Homestead Festival is the antique tractor and engine show put on every year by Gary Fletcher. When the festival was in its infancy, Lonnie Caudle would come from Brinkley with a semitrailer full of old hit-and-miss motors. He would set up in the driveway of Phil and Teressa's house for people to look at them. He did this for several years until the Homestead expanded. He decided not to bring them anymore because he didn't want to get dust and dirt all over his collection. Lonnie still attends every year if for nothing else than to get his annual supply of sorghum.

Around the same time Lonnie was pulling out, Gary Fletcher of the Bottomland Tractor Club in Caraway attended a festival and expressed an interest in coming the next year with some of his antique tractors. Gary and his stepfather, Bill Foster, took over the tractor show and set up in the barnyard each festival with several old tractors and other types of unique collections. It changes yearly. Some years, there are antique cars and old tools; other years there are bicycles. But Gary and Bill (up until his death) remain the heart of the show. Gary is now a part of our Homestead family and plans to convert part of the pole barn into a museum to house his collection of artifacts.

Granddad would have to get up several hours before they cooked to even get enough juice for a couple hours of cooking for the public. With the new mill, we can squeeze several trailers of cane and fill a five-hundred-gallon milk tank full of juice in less than an hour.

After the new mill was brought home, Cy had his chance to expand the pole barn. An additional fifty-two feet were added on the south side to house the mill. Looking at the pole barn now, you will see the mill and the sorghum cooking shed on the south side, storage in the middle and tractor and implement storage on the north side.

The new addition needed some more tin for the roof, and Cy found some old chicken houses around Conway that were no longer in use and had plenty of tin. After getting approval from the owners, Cy set off to get the necessary tin with his same three college friends—Steve Marsh, Roger Leder and Nick Martinez. Sometime during that day, Cy heard a loud noise from behind him on top of the roof. He looked around just in time to see Nick fall through the chicken house. Thankfully, Nick somehow managed to grab onto the roof on the way down and keep himself from falling all the way through. As Cy and Steve rushed to their friend's aid, they could see Nick's head, his knees and feet and both arms were still on top of the building, but his behind was through a large hole, and he was struggling to keep from falling the rest of the way through. Cy, Roger and Steve ran over and helped Nick up, and the three all climbed down to take a break. While standing on the ground, they heard a noise behind them again and looked just in time to see the entire chicken house collapse. They are all thankful that Nick went first so they didn't all fall through ten minutes later.

The pole barn is also the home to another disastrous claim to fame: during its construction, Trey Keller had the absolute worst wasp sting to the ear I have ever seen.

6
THE POST OFFICE AND PRINT SHOP

It just so happens that Teressa's uncle C. Edward Tudor, the same uncle who gave her the rope bed for Clark's Cabin, also had some pretty special press equipment. Uncle Eddie had in his possession an old George Washington hand press, manufactured on the East Coast sometime in the mid-1800s. Capable of printing single sheets up to twenty-four by thirty-six inches, it was used by Eddie's family up until about 1918.

Its history was very colorful, and not unlike that of many settlers to Arkansas at that time. The press was shipped up the White River by steamboat and then unloaded and hauled via wagon to Marshall, Arkansas, in the 1890s so that a Mr. William A. Wenrick could start himself a paper, the *Mountain Wave*. In 1928, Mr. James H. Tudor bought what was once the *Mountain Wave* (then known as the *Marshall Republican*) and acquired the press. The paper was handed down from James H. to his son James R. and then to James R.'s son Edward C. Tudor. When Uncle Eddie bought the paper, it was back to its original name, the *Mountain Wave*, and he published it up until his retirement several years ago. In the 1970s, Eddie sent the press to the Martin Box Market Craft Shop and Museum located a few miles north of Marshall.

Phil and Teresa wanted to expand the Homestead a little more and were looking at building a schoolhouse. When that fell through, Uncle Eddie contacted Teressa to see if she would be interested in the press but said she would need a building to house it. Phil and Teresa found themselves a building, built around the same time as the press, and purchased it from

The cabin that would become the Homestead post office in Bono, Arkansas, circa 1994. *Parker Family Collection.*

Harlan Hurd of Bono. The building was in a state of disrepair, but Phil had it renovated after about six months of work. And so the Homestead print shop idea was beginning to come to life.

The press was shipped to the Homestead in six pieces, and in August 1995, Uncle Eddie came to put it together. It took five men to carry the heavy cast-iron pieces inside the cabin and three together to hoist the heavy metal plate onto the press.

Uncle Eddie loaned the press (along with several sets of type) to Teressa with the understanding that if any of his kids wanted it, they had to give her six months' notice before they came and got it. Phil and Teressa set it up and began printing the "Pioneer Homestead Press" on it for groups of school kids and for the public at festival. After the press was housed in the Homestead post office and print shop for several years, Uncle Eddie told Teressa to forget about the loan—the press was hers.

Other objects on display in the print shop are several cabinets of handset type. While I was going to college, I met and became good friends with John Thomas of Jonesboro. He worked in the archaeology lab at Arkansas State, and I used to volunteer in there between classes. We became fast friends. After our fortuitous meeting, John started to work at Homestead

The Homestead post office and print shop flying the American flag on a crisp autumn day. *Parker Family Collection.*

School Kids, serving at one of the most beloved stations: teaching students about archaeology and Native Americans of Arkansas. Little did I know at the time, but his father (also John Thomas) was a retired journalism professor from Memphis State University (now University of Memphis). Mr. Thomas had many printing artifacts, including a lot of type. John secured the donation for the Homestead, and in the print shop it is. Teressa's Uncle Eddie also donated type, several gauges, work tools, a rare granite-topped printer's table and old photos of area newspaper and print shops.

Though pretty remarkable as a print shop, the building is not utilized solely for the George Washington press. While Phil was busy renovating the cabin, Tony Hoenick, formerly of Whitehall, decided to visit home and attended the festival. Tony's mother, Lois, used to be postmistress of Whitehall, and she had kept the old postal cage that was used from 1934 until 1966, when the post office was finally closed. The post office was at that time housed in the Hoenick Store. When Mrs. Lois died, Tony took the old postal cage to Santa Claus, Georgia. (Yes, that is really a place!) There the post office cage was used for letters sent to Santa.

After Tony came to the festival, he really wanted the postal cage returned to Whitehall and contacted Phil to see if he wanted it. Tony said

> ### Steamboats in Eastern Arkansas
>
> Items like the George Washington press coming into Poinsett County could not get here by water—it had to travel down the Mississippi River to Helena and then be unloaded and boarded onto a smaller vessel to come up the St. Francis as far north as Wittsburg (a town in Cross County that was thriving at the time but is no longer incorporated). After Wittsburg, the river simply gets too curvy and snaggy, making it dangerous for even an experienced riverboat captain to navigate. Everything was unloaded off the boats there at Wittsburg and put onto ox-driven wagons to head for all points north, including Whitehall, Harrisburg, Jonesboro and Paragould. The oxen teams would have to stay on top of Crowley's Ridge to avoid the swampy areas below, or they risked getting stuck. Mr. Joe Hall, an early resident who inadvertently gave Whitehall its name, bought lumber in Memphis to build his home. His lumber made its way to Whitehall just as described above—from Memphis to Helena to Wittsburg—and was then pulled by an ox team to Whitehall. He built a very impressive house with a large hall in the middle and painted it white. Locals called it the White Hall house, and later in 1882, when the post office was opened, residents petitioned to have the area called White Hall after Mr. Hall's famous house.

it belonged back home in Whitehall, and Phil enthusiastically agreed. So Tony donated the post office to Mark and Mike Morgan, whose parents, Don and Donna, leased the Hoenick farm, with the understanding that the Homestead would have a lifetime lease. Don, Donna and Mark drove to Georgia to pick up the post office and deliver it to the Homestead.

Not too long after that, Teressa was contacted by Whitehall resident Jimmy Foust with some interesting information. His mother, Helen Foust, had kept another Whitehall post office, which had been housed in the Foust Mercantile Store up until 1934, in her carport for some sixty years. Teressa did know about this post office, as Miss Helen had told her about it before. Ed Foust, Miss Helen's husband, was the postmaster in Whitehall until 1934. At that time postmasters had to purchase their own post office boxes, so they

Mr. J.C. Smith with the Parker Homestead George Washington Press. *Parker Family Collection*.

belonged to the individuals. So when he left the postal service, he took his postal cage with him.

Jimmy called Teressa after his mother passed away and asked if Teressa wanted his father's post office for the Homestead. Of course, Teressa said yes. The Foust postal cage could be the original postal cage in Whitehall, since the Whitehall post office was formed in 1882, and this one was used up until the mid-1930s; however, it is not known for sure if it does date to 1882 or if it came along later.

When the Homestead print shop and post office first opened up, it was not at all uncommon for locals to walk right in and put their old combination into a post office box and make it open, much to the delight of spectators. Both postal cages still have original mail in them that visitors to the Homestead can see. Perhaps one of the best pieces in the post office is a letter addressed simply to Jean, and it is marked, "Cancelled," meaning it was delivered. The Jean that the letter is addressed to just happens to be Phil's mother.

Mr. J.C. Smith, retired printer and pressman from Riverwood Carton in Memphis, had been helping with the sorghum station at the Homestead up until the post office and print shop was built. Since that time, he has printed papers and run the press for the Homestead. Teressa wrote the text and articles for the "Pioneer Homestead Press," and her Uncle Eddie had the plates made for J.C to print them with. As the prints are one of the favorite souvenirs at the Homestead each year, I cannot tell you how many people I have seen carrying around one of Mr. J.C.'s printed papers.

7
ROBERTS CHAPEL

When Teressa was a child, sometime before she was eight years old, her parents rented a house up on the ridge between Harrisburg and Greenfield down the road from the John Forbis family. She remembered playing with John's son Mike and also remembered that the Forbis family lived in a brick house. Interestingly enough, the log cabin that would become Roberts Chapel sat out behind their house (though Teressa doesn't remember that from when she was a child) and used to be their family residence.

John Wesley Forbis bought the land that had the log cabin on it from Fannie May (Clark) Guthrie when he moved to the Harrisburg area around 1960. Fanny May had moved back to Harrisburg and was running Guthrie's Grocery while taking care of her aging parents who lived in the cabin. Mrs. Margie Wright, who grew up down the road from the cabin, said most people referred to it and the land associated with it as "the old Clark place".

John's son Larry was in the third grade that year and remembered how the old cabin looked. He said it was set up as a three-room house, with a front room that was the living area, a middle room with a porch that was the bedroom area and a back room that was the kitchen. He remembers a wood-burning stove in the front room and that he and his brother, Mike (who Teressa remembers playing with), slept in the middle room.

Larry remembered the old cabin had siding on it and a tin roof, and he thought his parents must have slept in the front room. He also remembers a date, 1858, being carved in the log on the back right side. At any rate, his father was a carpenter, and their living in the old cabin was just temporary.

John Forbis moved the cabin from the old home site back into their eighty-acre cow pasture and then built the family's brick home on the site where the cabin once stood. So Teressa had familiarity with the old cabin's home place as a child, even though the cabin had been moved by the time she and her family lived out there, about 1965 or so.

Some years later, after his father's death, Larry relayed that his mother sold the pasture ground to Mr. Roberts with the old cabin still sitting right where his father had placed it. Roberts's son, Harold "Butch" Roberts, is who donated the building to the Homestead.

From Butch, we learned that Roberts Chapel was originally a two-room house, which is believed to have been built in 1858 by the Smith family. There is also an interesting Civil War story related to Roberts Chapel. The man who lived in the house was off at war, and his wife was home taking care of the farm. Union soldiers came by and took her only horse, a filly, and went off with it toward Cherry Valley. She was devastated. Despite this just being a mean thing to do, the soldiers had left a single woman running a farm without a horse, meaning she had nothing to work her fields with and would most likely lose all her crops. But fate intervened. According to local folklore, later that night, the woman heard a noise outside and went to investigate. The horse had escaped its captors and returned home.

During the winter of 1992–93, Butch asked Phil if he would be interested in coming to look at the old cabin. Butch told Phil that it was in almost complete ruin at that time and most likely beyond salvage, but Phil was still interested in coming to take a look. He thought at least he might be able to get a good log or two to use to patch a future cabin or maybe to make a bench, or he could possibly come up with some other way to reclaim the logs.

From the information he got regarding the condition of the cabin, Phil wasn't expecting too much. But once there, it turned out the logs were very sound, though the floor and roof were long gone. He was able to dismantle the cabin, bring it to the Homestead and set it right where it stands today, backed up against the Homestead creek.

The cabin was still covered in siding, which was very common. Many people who lived in log cabins were ashamed of that fact and would cover them with siding to hide their home's true origins. The siding oftentimes would help preserve the logs through decades where they would have otherwise started to rot. As Phil removed the siding he found something interesting carved into a log on the front right corner: the date 1858, Nov, that Larry Forbis remembered from when he was a child.

Roberts Chapel. *Parker Family Collection.*

> This excerpt from Mark Twain's *The Adventures of Huckleberry Finn* is quite telling of backwoods delta churches during the time period of Roberts Chapel, the 1850s and '60s:
>
> *Next Sunday we all went to church, about three mile, everybody a-horseback. The men took their guns along, so did Buck, and kept them between their knees or stood them handy against the wall…it was pretty ornery preaching—all about brotherly love, and such-like tiresomeness; but everybody said it was a good sermon, and they all talked it over going home, and had such a powerful lot to say about faith and good works and free grace and preforeordestination, and I don't know what all, that it did seem to me to be one of the roughest Sundays I had run across yet.*

Reconstruction lasted several months, and Roberts Chapel was officially dedicated May 29, 1994, in a service officiated by Reverend Captain Lovell. Looking around, every nail in the cabin was square, and the windows and doors were pegged. The poles in the gables of the building are the original rafters of the house and were able to be salvaged for their present use. Probably the most striking feature of the cabin is the beautiful stained glass. The windows, which allegedly came from the old convent in Jonesboro, were donated by Mr. John E. Roberts. He had them in his possession for many years in storage and decided that the chapel was just the place to put them. The building is named after "Mr. Johnny" as we called him and after Butch, thus it is Roberts Chapel.

Finishing out the unique décor are a couple pianos, several hymnals, some pews and a wood-burning stove for heat, which was donated by Phil's aunt and uncle Milton and Margaret Mann. One piano was donated by Gene Crouch of Harrisburg. The other was stuffed in a closet at Harrisburg High School until it made its way to Roberts Chapel. The hymnals came from Pleasant Valley Methodist Church (located just outside Harrisburg) and a couple of the pews came from the Whitehall Church of Christ and Lebanon Baptist Church of Whitehall. Mrs. Sylvia Condra donated the communion set, which was the older one from Pleasant Valley Methodist in Harrisburg. The beautiful doors out front were donated by Teressa's mother, Marion Westlake. She took them off her house and actually put up plywood at her residence until she could get new doors.

The pulpit is a cedar trunk from Phil's grandmother Lula Milam's old home place. Phil knew the tree was out there, dead, and had never been cut. Phil and Teressa always get very nostalgic about it, saying it was still there, almost like it was just waiting on them to come and get it. Cy remembered things a little differently. He said it was full of wasps when they cut it and caused everyone to take off running. But either way you remember it, the cedar pulpit in Roberts Chapel is breathtaking.

Phil and Teressa visited Silver Dollar City in Branson and loved the large picture window with the Bible verse above it in that city's church. They decided Roberts Chapel needed something similar. Phil got the large window donated from the Tri State Bank Building on Beale Street in Memphis, where he was doing construction work at the time, and Teressa began looking for the appropriate verse to put above it.

Nothing really hit her until someone brought by some old Sunday School pamphlets from 1936. Inside was the following verse:

> *The earth is the Lord's, and the fullness thereof; the world, and they that dwell therein.*
> *Psalms 24:1*

She instantly liked it, but she had so many verses going through her head. After all, this verse was going to be permanently etched in Roberts Chapel and it was not a decision to be made lightly. Later that week, Teressa said there was an old black-and-white movie on. She can't remember what it was or even who was in it. But there was a funeral scene, and that same verse from the Sunday School pamphlet, Psalms 24:1, was read out. She decided right then that Psalms 24:1 had been brought to her attention twice in a week for a reason. So she enlisted the help of Kyle Sanders, the Harrisburg agriculture teacher, who routed the words out for her, and her niece, Lexsi Mross, who painted it. Today, etched above the picture window in Roberts Chapel, you will find the abridged version of that verse.

Another unique artifact is located in front of the church: a headstone. Mrs. Thelma Barr called up Teressa to see if she wanted some headstones. I imagine Teressa was pretty silent waiting for Mrs. Thelma to explain the rest of the story.

During the flu epidemic of 1918–19, a boxcar load of headstones arrived one day at the Whitehall Depot. Because of the discrepancy between White Hall and Whitehall, the boxcar was sent to the wrong town. No one ever claimed any of the stones, and the railroad never picked them up. So the depot manager passed them out to people in the community to use as

Roberts Chapel, *Photography by Melissa Donner Photography at melissadonnerphotography.com.*

The headstone for an infant daughter of the Shearer family, dated 1919. *Parker Family Collection.*

Beautiful stained-glass window donated by John E. Roberts. *Photography by Melissa Donner Photography at melissadonnerphotography.com.*

steppingstones. Mrs. Thelma said many people in Whitehall came to get more than one headstone—some enterprising residents wanted to turn the inscribed stones around and use the backside for their future stones. Others used them as footings for their houses. Mrs. Thelma had two in her carport and asked Teressa if she wanted to come and look at them. She offered Teressa the smaller one and kept the big one—she was planning to use the back of it for her headstone (but of course her family did not do that).

When Teressa got over there she was surprised to see that the smaller stone had the family name of Shearer on it—"Grandpa Shearer," as the family refers to him, was Teressa's great-great-great-grandfather. So the stone you see in front of the church bearing the name Shearer does not mark a grave—it is actually an heirloom of a long-ago shipping mistake.

People often wonder if Roberts Chapel is still in use, and the answer is yes. Each year on festival Sundays, church is held inside. David Britnell and others will play the piano and lead singing, working magic on a piano that is not at all in a climate-controlled setting. Also, many churches hold all-day singings and picnics on the grounds at different times throughout the year.

A few years back, Pleasant Valley Methodist Church had a fire and was unable to use its church building, so the congregation came out to Roberts Chapel for about six weeks. At the end of their time in Roberts Chapel, the service was packed, and Teressa's grandmother Berneda Heeb declared they should just have church at Homestead every week. Teressa grew up attending Pleasant Valley, and she loved having them in Roberts Chapel.

Several weddings and vow renewals are held here each year. Phil's parents, Bob and Jean, had their fiftieth wedding anniversary in the chapel. The beautiful stained-glass windows are a focal point for almost every Homestead bride's wedding pictures, including mine.

8
THE GENERAL STORE

According to Steve Jernigan, the cabin that would become the Homestead general store was originally built in the 1920s. It was built by a barber as a hunting lodge. He worked in town (Harrisburg) on Fridays and Saturdays cutting hair, and during the week, he would go out to the cabin to hunt. It was also used to house farmhands and sawmill helpers one after another in succession up until about the 1960s, after which it sat abandoned.

Steve Jernigan donated the building to the Homestead, as it sat on his farm in the Weona area, off Buckhorn Road. Cy tore it down with some help from Steve Marsh, and they moved the logs to the Homestead. A three-room cabin, they put it back up just how it was with a couple aesthetic corrections. Cy had torn down another cabin in the Payneway area, and it was not in good enough shape to be used as a stand-alone building. He remembered tearing down that cabin explicitly, as it was in a cotton field, and he got the trailer stuck in the field, buried up in mud under the weight of the logs. I guess all is well that ends well, and after about three hours of waiting on someone to come pull him out, he got it home. They used the sound Payneway logs to patch the store where necessary.

While constructing the cabin, they called on Travis Easterling to come and help. They put the tin on the top, but it had a lot of holes in it that needed to be caulked. According to Travis, he did not know that was what he would be doing that day, and so he was wearing work boots. Phil had already caulked some of the holes, and the caulk was not dry. Travis quickly got to slipping and sliding up there and had to take off his boots and work

The cabin that would become the Homestead general store outside Weona on the Jernigan farm, circa late 1990s. *Parker Family Collection.*

barefoot. Phil tied a rope around Travis's waist and tied it to a nearby tree so that if he did take a tumble, he wouldn't go far. Phil and Teressa were telling me about this to put in the book and were both laughing pretty hard. And wouldn't you know it—Travis Easterling showed up at their house a couple days after they told me this story and told Teressa to get me to add to this story the fact that his bare feet were covered with tar, and he was like to never get them cleaned up.

Cy remembered more about the store construction, especially about the floors. What a lot of people don't think about is that Phil and Teressa are regular people who both have full-time jobs and all the bills everyone else has—a mortgage, car payments, a child—in addition to the financial

responsibilities of the Homestead. It would put a strain on just about anyone in their circumstance to replace all the flooring in their home. Well, Phil and Teressa had to put a floor in the store and, at the same time, had to have enough money left over for any kind of contingency that might happen in their personal household. Ever had a water heater got out unexpectedly? Had to replace an air conditioner? Imagine these unplanned costs after you have just put several thousand dollars into a gamble in your backyard—a gamble that people will continue to come and support the Homestead as it grows.

Phil went to a pallet mill on Highway 163 south and bought boards that were culls—not even good enough to be used for pallets. Well, that is not entirely true. Pallets are made out of leftover or culled boards that cannot be

The Parker Homestead General Store. *Parker Family Collection.*

Display inside Parker Homestead General Store. *Parker Family Collection.*

used for other purposes, but some of the boards that get culled at the pallet mill are simply thrown out because they are too wide. Sure, they are not ideal, but paying two dollars a board sounded good to Phil. If you go into the store today, Cy says you will notice knots, holes and just the general look of the floor in there is worse than all the floors in the other Homestead cabins.

One day after the store had been put back together, Tommye was out at the Homestead working on something while everyone else was away. A white-haired lady named Mrs. Mary Spears came walking up and said she understood that the house she had been born in was there—she was talking about the general store. Tommye took her over to it and let her in. She relayed many memories she had, such as her daddy throwing her into the air in the front room, where they slept, and what she and her brother played growing up. She also told Tommye that her mother roofed the house while pregnant with her and her twin brother. She said her daddy drank a lot, and her mother had to do most of the work. She remembered the loggers coming in to clear the trees and how her mother cried when her daddy sold the cleared land. She was very happy to see the cabin restored at the Homestead, and we are truly thankful to have her personal stories, which have added so much color to the general store's history.

Once all of the construction was finished, it was time to set it up. Teressa has many wonderful items of note on display, and each year, people try to buy them from her, but they are not for sale. For example, Cy says his favorite item we have on the entire place is the cigar lighter that sits on the counter. It came out of the old J.I. Foust store. The cash register came from Arthur Wallace, out of the old Wallace grocery store. Phil paid him five dollars for it, and when he got it home, there was a ten-dollar bill inside. The counter and big table came from Square Deal, and Josie Woodham donated the cabinet behind the counter. The "Drugs" sign came from Marshallene Prescott. Her father had Simmons Drug Store in Harrisburg, and she had been carrying the sign around in the trunk of her car until she saw Teressa at the grocery store, where she happily donated it to Teressa in the parking lot.

Jimmy Foust donated the coffee grinder. It came out of the old Foust store in Whitehall. He also called Teressa and asked if she would like to come over and go through any of his parents' things after his mother had passed away. They were trying to clean out but didn't want to throw anything away that might be of value to Teressa. She went over and sorted through trash bags and ended up getting enough bottles and items to fill up a cigar case that Mr. Johnny had given her. It sits on the store counter now with Mr. Ed's things on display.

Lye Soap Horrors

Early in our relationship, Cy took me to the Homestead for some reason. Maybe it was because he needed to pick something up at the house, I can't really recall. What I do remember is that his mother was cooking up a batch of lye soap.

Teressa was stirring lard in a large cast-iron cauldron with a boat paddle. It was boiling, and thick steam filled the air. She looked as if someone had tackled her to the ground and covered her with a one-inch-thick coat of Crisco, and I guess, in a way, that is what happened.

Over the years, I have gone with Teressa to a butcher shop outside Paragould that would save its leftover fat from hog processing for her. It is a nasty business all the way around I tell you. The first year Cy and I were married, I commented to him that out of everything there was to do at the Homestead, I just didn't think I would ever be able to make lye soap. He laughed and without hesitation informed me that he and his parents had a conversation about that very thing and that they came to the same conclusion.

Besides the grease and mess, there are several hazards associated with making lye soap. Teressa would go to our local grocery store and get Red Devil lye to make the soap with. One time, she went in and they didn't have any on the shelves. She asked management about it, and they said they had to put it behind the counter because it was a component in methamphetamine production. Luckily, they knew Teressa well and didn't mind ordering her all the lye she needed for Homestead soap.

On another occasion, Teressa had made all the soap she needed and had a lot of fat leftover. Earlier, Phil and Cy had dug a hole to put some construction leftovers in—pieces of boards and things of that nature—and they were going to burn it then cover it back up. Teressa didn't even think about it and had Cy to throw the pig fat in the hole with the wood. I think it must have rained, because Phil and Cy weren't able to burn the contents of the hole that weekend. As a matter of fact, I am not sure how much time passed before Cy was ready to go and burn them. He had his friend Nathan Thomas with him, and when they threw in the flame, an enormous explosion knocked them to the ground.

> I was in the house, maybe a quarter mile away, when it happened. I rushed into Caroline's room thinking she was hurt—the noise was so loud that I thought she must have knocked her television off the high shelf it was on. She looked at me like I was crazy, and I went back into the living room and just forgot all about it.
>
> A few minutes later, Cy and Nathan came staggering in the house looking worse for wear. Neither of them had any eyebrows, and they couldn't have heard thunder. Nathan said, "Why didn't you come to check on us!"
>
> Cy added, "We could be lying out there dead!"
>
> Nathan said, "We did lie out there for a while, and I thought I was dead!"
>
> They said people in Whitehall came from up and down the railroad tracks to see what in the world had exploded. We figured out later it was the rancid fat that caused the explosion, as it had melted and turned into nitroglycerin. Teressa apologized profusely, I made them some sandwiches and they staggered off together talking loudly. All these years later, Nathan still loves to tell that story.

The shelves came out of old Whitehall stores, along with a McCaskey filing system. There are antiques scattered throughout that are not for sale, but there are many other items in the store that are. Teressa has been making lye soap for years, and it is a staple in the store. There are Homestead cookbooks and coffee mugs, many home décor items and the ever-popular children's china tea sets and old-fashioned mixing bowl sets. My grandmother Mary Sue Redd (whom I called Sweet Mama) taught me to knit when I was nine or ten years old, and I make the hand-knitted dishrags that are for sale in the store using a pattern she taught me. There are just too many items in the store to list here, so you will have to come in and take a look for yourself.

9
THE BROOM SHOPS

The broom shop was actually the residence of Phil's great-great-grandfather Moses Pitts, who built it after returning home from the Civil War. Pitts was the last surviving Civil War soldier in Cross County. The building was torn down in the 1930s, and one wall from the residence was stored in a barn belonging to Phil's uncle Jerry Dan Milam. Always finding ways to use what they had, Phil and Teressa turned the one salvaged wall into an open-front cabin with a nice porch. This cabin would be immediately utilized to house another of the Parkers newly acquired treasures: the broom machine.

Phil obtained a broom machine in Green County through Tom Lovelace of Jonesboro. The machine was owned by Mr. Lovelace's brother-in-law, Raymond Atwood, and had been stored unused for more than sixty years.

The broom machine has an interesting history. It was patented in 1878 and made by the Boggs Broom Corn Co. of St. Louis. The machine was taken in lieu of debt by the late Moses Atwood in 1929, where it was stored unused until Phil got it in 1992. The equipment consists of three parts: the kicker machine, where the broom is actually put together; the broom press, where the broom is sewed; and the broom cutter, where it is trimmed up. Even though the machine is 135 years old at the time of this printing, it is in very good shape, in part due to the fact that it was unused for at least 63 years.

There is even more history to be found in the broom shed. One of our old broom hammers belonged to George Washington Spiegel. Spiegel was of the

The old Homestead broom shop, built with logs from Phil's great-great-grandfather Moses Pitts's home in Cross County, Arkansas. *Parker Family Collection.*

Harrisburg area and was a well-known broomsquire of his time. He raised his family in a three-room log house across the swan-pond ditch from Teressa's family farm. On Saturdays, his wife, Lottie, and their son, Sam, would load up a mule-drawn wagon and go out to peddle brooms. If the wagon was being used, they could carry about a dozen with them on their five-mile walk to town.

His brooms went for a quarter each until after World War II; then, he increased his price to thirty-five cents or three for a dollar.

It is a pretty interesting story about how the broom hammer came to the Homestead. Mrs. Vivian Sanders, one of our sorghum ladies, was moving to town. Her family had once lived in the old Spiegel place, and she called Phil and Teressa to see if they wanted to come and look through the old stuff she had before she moved and cleaned out. Phil immediately saw the broom hammer and had no idea what it could be. He asked what it was, and Mrs. Vivian told him it was Mr. Spiegel's old broom hammer. She let Phil have the broom hammer, and it was a wonderful find because Phil now had one of the essential tools to go with his broom machine.

The broom needle and thimbles came from James Frazey of Jonesboro. Mr. Frazey made brooms until the early 1940s, when he was no longer able to obtain the supplies needed due to wartime shortages. Both the needle and the thimbles were found in an old jar in an outbuilding behind his house—right where he put them when he closed up shop. And where did the cuffs that the broom thimbles are sewn into come from? Well, Teressa cut the tops off an old pair of Phil's work boots and took them along with the thimbles to the old shoe factory in Harrisburg, where they sewed them into broom cuffs for her.

Phil was very proud of his broom machine, though he had no idea how to use it. After word got out that the Parkers had a broom machine, a man showed up and pointed at it.

The man asked Phil, "Do you know what that is?"

Phil said, "I do! It's a broom machine."

The man said, "Do you know how it works?"

Phil said, "No, I don't."

> ## *Broom Making*
>
> Brooms are made out of a plant called broomcorn. It was imported to America by Benjamin Franklin in the 1700s specifically to use for brooms, though some florists use it as a background plant because of its beautiful color range. It takes about half an hour from beginning to end to make one Homestead broom. With two of us working together, we can make four to five an hour. At the end of an especially hard broom-making day, we may just make two or three an hour. Broom making, like blacksmithing, grist milling and many more of the "trades," were staples in small communities all across the United States until after World War II. At that time, mechanization and factories took over most of America's goods production.

The man who walked up that day was Buck Wolfe of Cherry Valley, who used to make brooms for a living. He and Leo "Pete" Rolland showed Phil and Teressa how to use their machine and that is how Homestead brooms were born. Homestead brooms are made just like brooms were made one hundred years ago, with the exception of the use of colorful broomcorn. Though Homestead brooms are more colorful, the broomcorn itself is the same stuff that would have been used. It has just been dyed into gorgeous colors in big vats, like Easter eggs on a larger scale.

We get a lot of questions about our broomcorn here at the Homestead. To answer the most asked one, yes, we have grown our own broomcorn at the Homestead before. It is a very versatile and easy crop to grow. The problem

The Parker Homestead kicker, patent date 1878. *Parker Family Collection.*

> **BEST SOUR CREAM AND GARLIC CHEESY BISCUITS**
>
> These are Caroline's favorite and taste very old fashioned. The garlic and cheese can be omitted and they taste like grandmas.
>
> *1 cup of sour cream*
> *2 cups of self-rising flour*
> *2 sticks of butter, softened*
> *½ cup of shredded cheese (I used cheddar)*
> *Sprinkle of garlic powder*
>
> Stir the first three ingredients together by hand until mixed. Do not over stir or the biscuits will not be fluffy. Add in the shredded cheese and the sprinkle of garlic and stir until just blended in. Scoop into a muffin pan, should make a dozen nicely sized biscuits.

is that you have to grow so darn much of it. We utilize our farm ground to raise sorghum and just order the broomcorn we need each year from a commercial broomcorn company out of Texas.

One of Teressa's favorite broom stories comes from a question posed to her at field trips. She said that when she and Phil were done demonstrating and asked kids if they had any questions, several times a day—without fail—a student would raise his or her hand and be called on only to point toward the sorghum mule and ask what his name was. Probably my favorite thing about making brooms for field trips is seeing Ms. Jennifer, a teacher from Westside. Each year, she comes over to give her testimony about how (as of this year) seventeen years ago, she bought a broom on her daughter's fourth grade field trip, and it is still in good shape. Phil and Teressa made that broom for her, and Cy and I have made her several since—one for her daughter's wedding and (funniest of all) one because she had redecorated her kitchen in new colors, and the broom she got from Phil and Teressa, though not worn out, did not match anymore.

Phil and Teressa were our broom makers from 1992 until 2004 when Granddad died. At that point, Phil got "promoted" to sorghum cook, and Cy and I got promoted from parking lot attendants to broom makers, which is where we are still stationed today. The funny thing about that promotion is that we were so happy to be out of the hot, dusty parking lot and just knew that anywhere we were placed would be better than there—that is, until we got stationed at brooms.

Teressa Parker teaching an enthusiastic and overwhelmed me how to sew brooms, circa 2002. *Parker Family Collection.*

I remember one fall when we were first learning, my Papaw and Granny, Louis and Martha Childers, were watching us intently. Cy and I were sweating and fighting the machines the best we could, hoping to have some sort of presentable output at the end of our efforts. Papaw grinned and told me he was so proud that I had "finally learned a trade."

Broom making is not an easy thing to do. The mechanics and instruction are not bad—we were taught in one afternoon. But the physicality of it is tremendous. Cy has a recurring back issue from an old college football injury, and I have a wrist injury from the police academy; together we limp along the best we can. We generally put on a good face and smile for the public, but I tell you once we get home after a very busy day of making thirty plus brooms, we are ready to take our ibuprofen and go to bed.

But broom making is not all bad. I have also been asked some very funny questions during field trips, such as the time a student pointed at Cy and asked me "Is he your Dad?" I got a lot of mileage out of that one, especially since I am actually three and a half years older than Cy. We used to ask students if they knew what old broom makers looked like and then sent them off to sorghum to look for Phil. On many occasions, they would come back to report to us that they thought old broom makers looked pretty rough. We laughed about this pretty hard the first two years we were making brooms and then suddenly thought to ourselves, "Oh gosh, we too will be old broom makers someday."

But despite all the hardships one encounters making brooms, our old broom shop was nestled under the trees, and on the very hot field trip days, we had the best spot on the whole place. Although there was the comfortable breeze, there were a few issues with our location. Since the cabin had an open-front set up, animals could (and often did) get in the broom shop and mess up our supplies. Cats loved to lounge around in the broomcorn Cy had spread out carefully to dry. We even had a hen named Mrs. McGee make a nest in there and sit one time! She had a particularly bad humor, and it did not make for a pleasant work environment for me or Cy, as we had to try to avoid a flogging while working along.

Though we had suffered through several irritations, Mrs. McGee was the last straw, and Cy began expressing his desire to have a new broom shop. He wanted one with a door he could close to keep the animals out. When the broom shop needed some structural repair work, Cy saw his chance, and we moved the broom operation up front and cater-cornered from where Clark's Cabin used to be into a cabin that had been set but not yet claimed.

The Homestead broom shop, circa 2013, *Parker Family Collection*.

The new broom shop is perfect. We still have shade, and best of all, we have doors that close. Not once have we had a chicken get inside and lay eggs in there. As for our old broom shop, Phil and Cy made the necessary repairs and our Homestead rope makers, Kenneth and Betty Brand, are pleased as punch to set up there. Of course, there are those that bemoan the fact that the rope makers inherited the cabin, but we just let them know, matter-of-factly that since their daughter Lesley Goad used to be the Homestead mayor, they may have gotten a little special treatment.

One funny story about getting the new broom shop is that Teressa told Cy about a cabin that he needed to go and get in Monette. So Cy, Phil, Caroline and I enlisted the help of our friends Seth and Mandy Whitmire and went to go get it. Once we arrived at Gathright Farms, it turns out "it" was "them." There were two cabins. That trailer was loaded down, and I mean loaded. I remember the back wheel wells on Cy's truck just almost touching his tires. We worked long and hard and finally ended up at Cracker Barrel to eat after a particularly dusty, dirty day. I know the people who were seated next to us had no idea we were the owners of Parker Homestead, and I am thankful for that.

We were all exhausted, none of us more so than Caroline, who was about six. She actually fell asleep at the Cracker Barrel table while lifting her fork up, and her head fell in her dinner plate. We quickly asked for a to-go box and left. On the way home, Phil called his dad, who was in the hospital at the time, and told him to look out the window to see the new cabins as we were driving by, and then he honked for him.

10

THE SMOKEHOUSE AND PICNIC AREA

When interviewing Phil and Teressa, I found out the smokehouse came from up around Piggott. A man named David Benson, who was friends with Teressa's sister Alyce, grew up in Piggott and his family had the cabin on their land. They donated it to the Homestead, and Phil remembered a terrifying trip hauling it home. Somewhere around Greenfield (about twelve miles north of the Homestead) he told Teressa he was about to lose the load all over the highway. As he was telling me this story, Teressa questioned him, saying, "Are you sure it was the smokehouse and not another cabin? It's a small one! I remember that time but I can't imagine it being the one we almost lost."

Phil was quick to reply in the affirmative. He said yes he was sure that was it, and added, "When you don't have a very substantial trailer, and you don't have a very good truck to haul the trailer with…" I understood exactly what he meant.

A few years back, Cy and I went to Sam's Club in Jonesboro to pick up a pallet of bottled water for the festival. They were supposed to have it shrink-wrapped and palletized for us, ready to put on the trailer. When we got there, the water was wrapped, but was leaning hard to one side. I told Cy, "I think that looks awfully wonky. Should we ask them to rewrap it?" He brushed me off and said it was fine. You know how far we made it with that pallet of water? We tried to pull out of the parking lot and go straight across Caraway Road to McAlister's deli and lost about a third of the water in the road, not twenty feet out of the Sam's parking lot.

Parker Homestead

The Homestead smokehouse. *Parker Family Collection.*

I told him it looked wonky.

Strangely enough, losing a pallet of water on one of the most-traveled roads in Jonesboro was not the worst part of our day. On the way home and just a little after lunchtime, we stopped on Senteney Road in Greenfield to look at a cabin someone had called us about. It was right off the gravel road- we didn't have to drive through private property or anything like that. We parked and walked over to look. The cabin was in bad shape, had rounded logs that were small and Cy decided pretty quick it would not be something we were interested in.

Turning around to walk back to the truck we met a man pulling up to us who promptly pulled out a gun and asked what we were doing there. Cy calmly explained who he was and that we were there to look at the cabin while I held onto his arm for good measure. The man put his gun away then asked us if we were just in Jonesboro. Cy said yes, and the man told us he saw the pallet of water fall as we went across the road and that he thought to himself that it was way too hot to be out in the middle of the highway picking up one thousand bottles of water.

I thought so, too!

So as you can see, we have gotten ourselves into some pretty crazy situations over the years while "Homesteading." When Phil relayed the story

Washing and hanging out, a lye soap demonstration by Tommye Rosa. *Parker Family Collection.*

about the smokehouse, I more than understood what he was talking about. Somehow they did make it home with those logs and set it up at the top of the picnic area right across from the general store.

Phil's aunt Martha Milam told me a story about the smokehouse her parents had when she was growing up. She said every fall, they would butcher a hog and that during the winter, her mother or grandmother would ask her to go out to the smokehouse and cut off a piece of ham or bacon and bring it in for them to cook. She said it would go on this way until spring, and when she would be sent out to fetch another piece, there might be maggots on it. She would cut off the ham as instructed and they would soak it in saltwater to cleanse it before cooking. But she said that once the maggots showed up on the meat they knew that it was getting a little too warm to be using the smokehouse.

Teressa said Ms. Sylvia Condra had a similar story about the smokehouse of her youth. That kind of living might make the faint of heart a bit queasy, but for people growing up during those times, it was a way of life. Teressa said Ms. Sylvia got food poisoning one time, she thought when Sylvia was in her 80s. (Phil said he thought it was when she was in her 90s.) At any rate, Mrs. Sylvia told the doctor that she had no idea why she got sick because she

Cajun Etouffeé

While I am busy making brooms, my sister and friends have set up for years selling my Cajun étouffée. The name comes from the fact that all the étouffeé I had ever tried was of the crawfish variety, but I wasn't always able to get my hands on crawfish out of season. So when my family had a hankering for some étouffeé, we just got creative and made it anyway—with chicken and shrimp. OK, so maybe chicken and shrimp isn't so Cajun, but a few years back, I actually had a French-speaking Cajun come up and kiss me after she tried it at the festival. I couldn't really understand what she was trying to tell me, but the kiss said it all. Hope you enjoy as much as she did. Elizabeth Childers, Carrie Johns and Kathy Evans can tell you from their festival experiences that you won't have any leftovers. This is my all-time most requested recipe, hands down.

I use 2 cans of chicken broth, but if you prefer the roux to be thicker use 1 or 1½. This recipe should serve six to eight (depending on how many Cajuns are in your group), and I cook about one and a half cups of rice (3 cups cooked) to go with it.

1 sticks butter, plus ½ stick
½ cup all-purpose flour, plus extra, if needed
1 cup chopped yellow onion
½ cup chopped green bell pepper
1 cup chopped celery
3 cloves garlic, finely minced
½ teaspoon black pepper
½ teaspoon cayenne pepper, more if desired
1 teaspoon Cajun seasoning
½ cup minced green onions, plus extra for garnish
½ cup minced fresh parsley leaves
Dash hot sauce (optional)
1 or 2 cans chicken broth
1 (14.5-ounce) can diced tomatoes, such as Rotel
Salt, if needed
3 chicken breasts, boiled and shredded
2 handfuls of medium shrimp, 31/35 size preferably (substitute crawfish for shrimp if in season)
Cooked rice

Make the roux by melting the stick of butter in a large heavy saucepan over low heat and then adding flour. Whisk flour to form a paste. Continue cooking over low heat and whisk continuously until the mixture turns a caramel color and gives off a nutty aroma, about 15 to 20 minutes. To the

> roux, add the onion, green pepper, celery and garlic and cook over low heat for about 5 minutes, until the vegetables are limp. Add the black pepper, cayenne pepper, Cajun seasoning, green onions, parsley and hot sauce (optional) to taste. Add the chicken broth and the tomatoes with their juice. Stir to blend. Add the salt, starting with 1 teaspoon, and then add more if needed. Bring the mixture to a boil. Then reduce the heat to low and simmer for 10 to 15 minutes. Add cooked and shredded chicken breast and stir. After the étouffeé smells wonderful (about 5 minutes after chicken is added in), add the shrimp. It will take about 3 minutes for the shrimp to cook. Don't overcook. Remove from heat. Add the remaining ½ stick butter and stir; the heat from the dish will melt the butter. Serve over rice, with extra Cajun seasoning for those who desire a little more heat.

cut all the green off the sausage before she cooked it. Ms. Sylvia lived to be 102 years old, so maybe their way of thinking was not all that bad.

Directly behind the smokehouse is the picnic area. Many things have taken place back there over the years. During School Kids, the washing station is set up there, and kids learn all about washboards and lye soap. Quilting has also been set up down there, and before Aunt T got her building, she set up down there with kettle corn.

During festival the picnic area is the place to be to get some great food. Beans and cornbread have been served by the Bay Village Assembly of God for years, and they are great. First-time festivalgoers always ask what the long line is for and are shocked when they find out it's for beans and cornbread. Also in the picnic area is barbeque, which has been served by several different people over the years, including Tommy Dobson, the Poinsett Masonic Lodge 184 and most recently by Sean and Cori Hammond of Harrisburg. It is always fantastic.

Rounding out the food are two stops right up the hill from the picnic area. The first is pork rinds by James Cunningham. They generally sell out each day, and he also brings the best corn on the cob I have ever had. I stay pretty busy making brooms during festival and don't "get off the porch" to eat much of anything. But I always send someone with some money to get me some of James's corn. The other famous food stop is the Homestead fried pies station. Our daughter, Caroline, and her cousin Maddi Mross started their own fried pie business in 2010, getting a $1,000 loan from the bank as two twelve year olds, and they were able to pay it back in full after that festival. The girls have been able to be their own bank ever since. Chocolate and peach usually sell out right after lunch, so if those are your flavors, be sure and visit the fried pies stand early.

Many times when festivals are advertised, one of the main draws is the food, and the Homestead Festival is no exception. We are proud of our great food vendors, and thankful they are here!

Teresssa's cousin Vickie Winningham was the original witch for the Haunted Homestead. She would set up in the picnic area next to Roberts Chapel and offer people to sit down and rest a bit, take a deep breath and decide if they wanted to continue the scary tour or just give it up. Many children (as well as adults) would bail out right there after the scare up front.

Vickie had a table full of Halloween props, including a kettle full of witch's brew. She would greet visitors and try to assure them that they had already made it through the worst part. To the side and behind the witch's station was another fire, which was set up for the workers to roast hot dogs, take a break and just be spectators. One night, after things had slowed down, Vickie and Annetta Reddmann were sitting there relaxing and talking about how the night had gone. David and John Wallace just happened to be walking through, and David remarked what a good fire Vickie and Annetta had going down there. And they sure did. The hay-bale seating had caught on fire and had ignited loose hay that was spread on the ground. Vickie was high stepping it, hopping around and trying to beat it down with her witch's broom. Annetta was trying to smother it with a blanket. The only problem was that their efforts were doing little but fanning the flames and making the fire spread even more. Water hoses were quickly brought to task, and the danger to the Homestead was averted.

11

THE KETTLE CORN SHED

Located right between fried pies and pork rinds, to the east of the church, is the kettle corn shed. Teressa's aunt Tommye Rosa, or "Aunt T," runs the operation, though she didn't start out popping kettle corn at all. Tommye's first job at the Homestead was as a runner—she would answer the phone at the house during the festival, or if a problem arose, she would run over to Phil and Teressa where they were making brooms, let them know what was going on and then go handle it according to their instructions. One year, Tommye got to talking with Mr. Cliff Burns. He brought roasted peanuts and sarsaparilla to sell at the early festivals. While they were talking, he mentioned other festivals and events he went to and how he had to haul a trailer everywhere because of his sarsaparilla. Then as a kind of second thought he casually stated that "the kettle corn guy doesn't have to—all he has is popcorn, salt, sugar and oil."

That got Tommye thinking. The Homestead didn't have a kettle corn guy. Maybe she could do kettle corn for the Homestead.

Tommye did some reconnaissance. She and her daughter Brooke watched a man popping kettle corn at Heber Springs. She watched him for a long time. And before too long, she thought she might be ready to try. Aunt T bought a kettle for seventy-five dollars, and Allen Mathews of Harrisburg built her a frame to put it in. At first, she would experiment and bring some to the courthouse for her coworkers to try. After she thought she had it about right, she asked Teressa if she thought that kettle corn might work at the Homestead.

> ## Sassafras Tea
>
> Look around the kettle corn shed and the church, and you will surely see several sassafras trees. Sassafras was used for many things, but especially to make tea. It is claimed to have medicinal values, and you can still find sassafras extract in health-food stores today. Try planting monkey grass anywhere in the area around the church or kettle corn shed, and your shovel is bound to hit a root or two; the scent is overwhelming. It is like fresh root beer floating up.
>
> Teressa's Uncle Eddie drank sassafras tea as a boy for a "tonic," and the last time he visited Phil and Teressa, he got some of the bark to take home with him. He called Tommye and told her the tea he made out of it was as good as he remembered.
>
> *4 pieces of sassafras bark*
>   (*or several pieces of roots*)
> *5 cups of water*
>
> Wash bark (or roots) and place in water. Boil. Color of water will change, and you just taste to judge the strength. Do not dilute! Drink it hot and sweeten as needed with honey.

When Aunt T first starting popping at the Homestead, she didn't have a building. During School Kids, she popped in the picnic area under the old arbor, where the beans and cornbread sets up at the festival now. At the festival, she would pop in front of the little barn. She relayed a pretty funny story to me about popping kettle corn there. She was popping up batch after batch during a festival several years back, and as she had a batch done, she would pour it into a large black cauldron. Teressa's nephew Dakota Tucker was about three or four, and Tommye saw him making his way toward the cauldron, carrying a handful of leaves and sporting a mischievous look on his face. Though Tommye knew what he was about to do she couldn't put down her paddle to leave the very hot popping corn with a crowd and get to him in time. She had to watch helplessly as Dakota dumped all the leaves into the big pot (which was about two thirds full of kettle corn) with a huge smile of accomplishment. Of course, they had to dump all of that kettle corn out and start over. I told her that was a pretty funny story; she said not so much at the time.

Tommye is not sure exactly how it happened, but eventually, she got her own building. It came from Steve Jernigan's farm outside Weona, and whether she knew

Tommye Rosa in her kettle corn shed. *Parker Family Collection.*

about it and asked him to have it or whether he offered it to her out of the blue she can't quite remember. In any event, she was proud to have it. Steve said the house had been vandalized, and when she got there, she could see what he was talking about: there were .22 bullet holes all throughout the front, like someone had set up on the road and used it for target practice. In its earlier days, the kettle corn shed was once a two-room cypress house with a great room and a lean-to kitchen. There is no definite date about when it was built, but it had been vacant since 1950. It was about 1998 that she went to get it and set it up at the Homestead.

Cypress is very valuable wood and, at the time the kettle corn shed was originally built, was in abundant supply in this area of Arkansas. Cypress boards are expensive and rot resistant, mainly because the trees prefer to grow in swampy areas. That particular quality in cypress is what makes it last so long

Sweet Potato Biscuits

One of the stories Tommye shared with me was about sweet potato biscuits. In the olden days, when flour would start to run low toward the end of winter, mashed sweet potatoes would be added to biscuit dough as a flour extender. The biscuits would have small flecks of orange in them, but there wouldn't be much difference in their taste. As a treat, hot sweet potato biscuits were sliced up and spread with fresh butter before being topped with heavy cream that had been whipped up with a small amount of honey, which sounds wonderful to me.

4 tablespoons butter
¾ cup cooked and mashed sweet potatoes
⅔ cups milk
1¼ cup plain flour
4 teaspoons baking powder
1 tablespoon sugar
½ teaspoon salt

Mix butter into potatoes and stir in milk. Sift the flour. Then, sift again with remaining dry ingredients. Stir the flour mixture into the potato mixture. Turn the dough out on a floured board and toss lightly until smooth. Pat down to about ¾-inch thick, cut out and bake at 450 degrees until done, about 12 to 15 minutes.

---

where other woods will decay. The boards on the kettle corn shed, especially in the corner, are very wide. Tommye said she was especially careful with those because she could not imagine a tree that size. The back door of the shed was the original kitchen door of the house, and if she will let you, be sure to look at the inventive door lock. It is a piece of wood that turns sideways to bar the door. The floors, porch and window casings are original to the old house as well, and the room itself is half of the "great room" Tommye found when she originally acquired the cabin.

Now Aunt T is not going to let me give away her recipe here, but she does want me to tell you that kettle corn should have a light, sweet taste. Sugar was rare in pioneer times, and they would not have doused their popcorn in it. Kettle corn was used for special occasions or treats and would oftentimes be popped at events like church socials or hog killins, both of which Tommye has popped for.

She said that no one is for sure how the recipe or idea came about, but maybe after a hog killin, there was a little lard left over. Perhaps since everyone was together, someone decided to use that lard and a little bit of salt and sugar and throw

Collin McCrary and Caroline Parker in their wedding finest, just a few minutes before they jumped in the creek. *Parker Family Collection.*

some popcorn in it. However it got started, it is a wonderful treat that people still enjoy and one of the most popular stops at Parker Homestead.

Not only is the kettle corn shed popular for the kettle corn, but it is also a wonderful spot to get into the creek. When Cy and I got married in 2003, Caroline, age five and our flower girl, and Collin McCrary, our six-year-old cousin and ring bearer, disappeared shortly after the ceremony. Everyone was busy taking pictures and hugging family and friends, and no one had eyes on

Popcorn Balls

1 cup brown sugar
½ cup dark corn syrup
½ cup sorghum syrup
1 tablespoon butter
1 tablespoon vinegar
2 gallons popped corn

Boil sugar, corn syrup, sorghum and butter together until the mixture becomes brittle when tested in cold water. Add vinegar and remove from heat. Gradually but quickly, pour the syrup over the popcorn and stir until all the popcorn is coated. While still warm, butter your hands and roll into balls. Store in a dry place at room temperature.

---

the young wedding attendants. I don't remember who it was that found them, but I do remember that they were dragged back to the ceremony sopping wet with their nice wedding clothes covered in mud. They had slid down the bank behind the kettle corn shed and were playing in the creek. This is why the pictures of our reception have the kids in play clothes. To this day, the kettle corn shed is still a favorite spot for the kids to get in the creek and play.

12

THE BLACKSMITH SHOP, THE SARSAPARILLA SHED AND JULIE BELL'S BARN

Phil started really wanting a blacksmith shop immediately after he and Teressa talked about expanding past Clark's Cabin. His first go at it was a simple anvil and forge, which he set up out in the open right past the little barn. He wanted a real shop though, so he built a small building about the size of the ticket booth we now have standing at the front gate. He put his blacksmith things in there and was so happy until Teressa threw him out.

She had printed a cookbook and wanted a small store, so she happily used the makeshift blacksmith building and set up shop. But Phil would not be deterred. He and Teressa began making plans and trying to decide how to make the new blacksmith area. One day while driving down Southwest Drive in Jonesboro, Bennett's nursery caught their eyes. The nursery had a nice building in a barn shape with two open doors on the front. Phil immediately liked it for his blacksmith shop.

They measured the building, got the materials necessary and built it at the Homestead. The new and improved blacksmith shop was open for business. Phil had it all set up just like he wanted it, and business was good. It was about that time that Mr. Cliff Burns, the man who gave Tommye the idea about kettle corn and the man who had been bringing sarsaparilla to the early festivals, moved. Teressa immediately thought she could sell sarsaparilla, but she needed a building.

So Phil's second building and third attempt at a blacksmith shop was taken away, and the sarsaparilla shed was born.

Mama Sue's Chocolate Cake

Bertie Sue Parker, or "Mama Sue," was Granddad's mother, and she was an excellent cook. She would make cakes to sell for holidays and special occasions, and her goodies were very popular. So much so that she made enough money selling cakes to buy a car. Here is one of our favorite Mama Sue recipes.

Cake

1 cup water
½ cup oil
1 stick oleo (margarine)
2 tablespoons cocoa powder
2 cups flour
1 teaspoon baking soda
Salt (to taste)
2 cups sugar
2 eggs
½ cup buttermilk
Vanilla extract, to taste

Icing

1 stick oleo (margarine)
3 tablespoons cocoa powder
6 tablespoons buttermilk
Pinch salt
Vanilla extract, to taste
1 (16-ounce) box powdered sugar

Cake: In a medium saucepan, heat water, oil, oleo and cocoa powder until oleo is melted. Meanwhile, in large mixing bowl, combine flour, baking soda and salt. Pour heated mixture over dry ingredients, beating well. Add eggs, buttermilk and vanilla. Pour batter into greased cake pan. Bake at 350 degrees until done (knife or toothpick inserted comes out clean).

Icing: Melt oleo, cocoa powder, buttermilk and salt in a medium saucepan. Remove from heat. Add vanilla and powdered sugar. Beat well, and add nuts if desired.

On busy days, workers in the sarsaparilla shed can barely keep up with demand. With two workers filling orders and one constantly restocking the drink boxes with drinks and ice, it is all they can do to keep the lines that are forming at bay. I speak from experience—I worked the sarsaparilla shed for several years before I moved up to broom making.

One year, our neighbor Lynn Denton set up selling frozen yogurt next to the sarsaparilla shed during School Kids. It was a particularly hot day, and both the drink shed and the frozen yogurt stop were slammed. Lynn had to run a quick errand and asked me if I could take over for a few minutes. A man stepped up with his grandson and said to me, "My goodness lady, they are working you to death! You parked our bus, took our group to a station, sold me a drink, took the trash out of the restrooms and now you're selling ice cream!" I still laugh thinking about it.

Speaking of laughing, Teressa was laughing pretty hard while telling me the sarsaparilla shed origins and how she "stole" it from Phil. She said that where the sign hangs that says "Sarsaparilla Shed" there used to be a sign that said "Blacksmith." She still has the sign and said she would show it to me.

Poor Phil—after all this defeat you would think a man would just give up. But he would not give up on the dream. Using the extra logs left over from constructing the big barn (the logs that came from the old American Legion Hut in Trumann) Phil made his third blacksmith building and fourth blacksmith attempt. Teressa wants me to point out that she hasn't taken it away, yet.

Every festival and School Kids event, the blacksmith shop is up and running, with Carl Steyer and his brother Martin doing demonstrations and making courting candle holders, fire pokers and even artwork. One year, Carl made Teressa a set of sorghum stalks that are absolutely beautiful. She treasures them.

In between the blacksmith shop and the sarsaparilla shed is an animal pen and barn with a sign reading, "Julie Bell" on it, which was presented to us by Charlie McClain. Julie Bell is the Homestead donkey and is very popular. Julie Bell has been featured on the news and in the newspaper and is one of the most popular stations on field trips. Homestead donkey Julie Bell is joined by a rotating cast of farm animals every year—just whatever we are raising at the time. In years past, we have showcased Belted Galloway calves, turkeys, peacocks, goats, ducks, pigs, chickens, guineafowl, miniature horses, sheep, kittens, rabbits and many more animals.

One of our more beloved animals that was also featured in the newspaper was our pig Snicky. Snicky was named after Cy's friends from college Steve Marsh and Nick Martinez. Snicky was Julie Bell's constant companion—they were totally bonded, and we are not sure to this day whether Snicky thought he was a donkey, a dog or what.

As a matter of fact, a few festivals were even disrupted a bit because of Snicky's affinity for anything equine. When Papa Chuck and Mike

Carl Steyer, Homestead's blacksmith. *Parker Family Collection.*

Henderson would bring in their horse teams to run the covered wagon rides, Snicky would affectionately chase the horses around the barnyard and rub up on their legs. Obviously this made the horses that did not hold pigs in high esteem quite nervous, and we had to take measures to confine Snicky (generally a free-range pig) so that he couldn't get over there and bother them. He was simply devastated penned up until we put Julie Bell in the stall with him. They were really quite the pair.

Julie Bell

The Haunting Donkey

Julie Bell, trying to get in the general store with Teressa and Tommye. *Parker Family Collection.*

Teressa and Tommye were working in the store one night, setting up displays and straightening up for the next day. It was late at night, but with the lights on in the store and work to do, the pair didn't have time to be scared by being out in the Homestead after dark. That is until they heard footsteps on the general store porch.

"Did you hear that?" they asked each other. They wondered who could it be. As far as they knew, everyone was asleep. They stood there for a minute and listened but didn't hear the sound again, so they went back to work cautiously. And that was when they heard it again.

Teressa and Tommye linked arms and slowly snuck to the door. They looked out, and lo and behold, Julie Bell, the Homestead donkey, was looking at them. She wanted in and was walking up and down the porch. When she saw them, Julie Bell stuck her face right up to the window and brayed loudly. When Tommye opened the door, Julie Bell tried to get in, so they had to push her back to close it. Teressa told Tommye she wasn't quite finished, so Tommye found a pack of gum off the counter and cracked the door to give a piece to the donkey.

This seemed to work for a time, and when Julie Bell got more insistent, Tommye would open the door and give her another piece of gum. Finally, Tommye told Teressa she was going to have to hurry up because she was almost out of gum and couldn't hold Julie Bell back much longer. So they called it a night and put Julie Bell back to bed before going up to the house themselves. Another funny outcome from that night was that Teressa actually took pictures of the attention-starved Julie Bell trying to get in the store that night and made postcards out of them.

13

THE GRISTMILL

In the Homestead's beginnings, Phil and Teressa just knew they would need a gristmill. A gristmill was an important part of any rural community, and oftentimes the local residents would band together to help build and support their local mill. Once set up and running, area farmers would bring in their corn or other grains to be ground up and would leave with the finished product of meal or flour to use for baking. With bread as such an important staple of early pioneer's diets, every community needed a gristmill.

The Homestead's first gristmill came from up on the ridge and was bought from Charlie Worley for ten dollars. Phil was excited to have it. He brought it home and placed it under the lean-to on the little barn. After some time, he decided to build a small shed for it, and as the Homestead continued to expand, Phil built another even larger shed to house it—this one backed up to the creek.

One day, Mrs. Thelma Barr called and said that her parents' home, which was located on Phil and Teressa's road (maybe a quarter mile from their house), was about to be sold. She informed them that her parents' old store, known as the Foust Store, stood right next to the house and the slab from the store was still there. A little further into the story, she let them know that the old gristmill out of her parents' store was still there, between the house and the railroad tracks, and that they should go get it before the house sold.

Phil and Teressa were pretty much flabbergasted. They had driven right past it all those years and didn't even know it was there. They went to search for it, and sure enough, it was surrounded by hedges and brush and weeds—but it was there.

> ## The Homestead Cornbread Recipe
>
> 1½ cups stone-ground cornmeal
> ½ cup flour
> ½ teaspoon salt
> 4 teaspoon baking powder
> ¼ cup sugar
> ¼ cup oil
> 1 cup milk
> 1 egg
>
> Mix dry ingredients and then add remaining ingredients, stirring well. Fill greased pan, cast-iron skillet or muffin pan half full. Bake at 425 degrees for about 25 minutes or until lightly browned.

Tim Murphy had a four-wheel drive truck and came over with a chain to pull it to the Homestead, and before too long, Phil and Teressa had a much larger and nicer mill, one that actually was in operation right by the Homestead. It was an awesome find. Curt Hodges once relayed a story about the mill when it was still in operation. He said Whitehall residents would generally bring their corn to be ground on Saturdays, and one such day, several men were sitting around and waiting their turn when another gentleman came in and exclaimed, "Why, I could eat that meal as fast as that thing can grind it!"

William Joiner happened to be in the room at the time and asked the man, "How long could you hold out?"

The man replied, "'Til I starved to death!"

A new larger shed was built to house the old mill, and it was set up to run using a tractor and the old line shaft from the old Whitehall cotton gin, donated by Carl Woodham. The mill makes a wonderful racket when in operation. I remember being a good distance away at field trips when it went off one year. You didn't really know from a distance that you were hearing the humming of the gristmill until you weren't. Quite a few times over the years, Cy and I would be on a trash run, leading out a group, selling sarsaparillas or what have you when the noise would stop. We would simply excuse ourselves and take off to the gristmill to get it going again.

Once in the early years, the gristmill broke down, and David Reeves came out to help. According to Cy, David worked on it for most of a day, and when he got it back up and running, he would not let Phil pay him for his help. Cy said this was early on, at a time when Phil and Teressa didn't have many tools or things to work with.

Though the new larger shed was quite picturesque, being backed up against the creek posed a problem. The majority of the year, the creek bed

Parker Homestead's old gristmill building, housing the newer mill that came out of the Foust Store in Whitehall. *Parker Family Collection.*

is either dry or has a trickle flowing in it. But when we get a good rain of a couple inches or more, everything drains into the creek, and it leaves its banks. Generally, once a year or more, the gristmill would be inundated with water and several things would float out, not to mention all the sticks and debris that would float in. So a few years back, we moved the gristmill one more time up onto higher and dryer ground.

In 2004, we acquired a cabin from Gathright Farms in Monette. The Dudley barn, as it was called, had originally been used as a corncrib by the William Dudley family, and Phil and Cy reconstructed it for use as the new gristmill building at the Homestead. They built a shed onto the side of the Dudley barn and then added a nice wraparound porch. And up against the split-rail fence at the edge of the parking lot is where the gristmill now sits. I know Gary McClain, our miller during the festival each year, and Donnie Ray Winningham, Teressa's cousin and our School Kids miller, will tell you they are proud of the new building. Other grist millers, such as Mandy Whitmire, Annetta Reddmann and James Frazey, have also helped out through the years. The Homestead gristmill grinds stone-ground cornmeal at both the festival and the School Kids events, as well as a few other times

The new Parker Homestead gristmill. *Parker Family Collection.*

throughout the year for special purposes, such as for the local Girl Scout troop to bag up cornmeal for the food pantry.

Homestead cornmeal is the only cornmeal I have used for the past eight or so years save one time when I ran out and had to buy some at our local grocery store. It was very soft, almost a flour consistency, and not at all what I had grown accustomed to. I will never run out again. Several acquaintances of mine have asked me to please get them some over the years. There is just no substitute for stone-ground cornmeal, period.

Another use we have for the gristmill is the skeet-shooting station. We love to get together with friends and all of our kids and shoot skeet. The building provides shade for us, and the skeet thrower can sit under it and shoot right out to the parking lot. It is a perfect location and has been utilized many, many times. We have also had scouts set up there to shoot archery and BB guns.

Be sure and notice the cabin that sits to the east of the gristmill. This is the Bay cabin, and we currently use it as a produce shed. It was also the site of a Farm Bureau *Front Porch* magazine photo shoot featuring my family.

I remember going with Cy to get this cabin, which was located in the middle of town in Bay, sitting behind a modern residence in a small backyard. The owners of the residence were trying to get it certified to be HUD housing, and for some reason, the housing authority did not want a dilapidated cabin in the backyard. So we went and got it, set it up there in the corner and it is, as of now, unfinished. Brad Beetch and Travis Eddleman helped put the roof on, and we still laugh about that experience.

It does have a roof and floor, but we have not gotten any further than that. I suggested to Cy that we could make it into a barbershop (Teressa got an awesome antique barber chair from Phil one year for Christmas) or maybe the Homestead jail, but he says that Teressa wants to make it into another cabin people can stay in. She wants to eventually have five cabins out back: one for her and Phil; one for me and Cy; and one each for Caroline, Kyra and Kaiser to come home to stay in.

14

THE E. SLOAN HERITAGE SCHOOL

The eighth building added to the Homestead was the E. Sloan Heritage School, which was donated by Betty Sloan of E. Sloan Farms out of Jonesboro. Teressa had been thinking about putting in a schoolhouse for some time, and before the building was even secured, items began pouring in. Mrs. Katherine Furnatter of Harrisburg had been a teacher for fifty years and worked with Teressa at the elementary school. The last spring she taught, she came to Teressa and told her to come and look through her things to see what the Homestead might be able to use once the schoolhouse was built. Teressa picked out several things from Mrs. Furnatter, and they are prominently on display today.

Another day at the elementary school some old readers were being set into the hall. Teressa said they were fair game for anyone, teachers or students, to pick through before they ended up being thrown away. She got several, and they are also inside the schoolhouse. Another thing from the elementary school was an old map the fourth grade teacher threw out. It was badly out of date and had been replaced, and Teressa got it out of the trash.

Yet another treasure recovered from Harrisburg Schools is a simple piece of cardboard. Mr. Lloyd Lackey, superintendent of Harrisburg Schools at the time, called Teressa one day because of a unique piece of cardboard found in the school district bus shop. You may be thinking who cares about a piece of cardboard, but this one is pretty unique.

When the Whitehall School was closed and consolidated into Harrisburg School District, the actual school building was moved to

Inside the E. Sloan Heritage School. *Photography by Melissa Donner Photography at melissadonnerphotography.com.*

School books and a lamp sit on the teacher's desk. Notice the jelly bucket in the corner. *Photography by Melissa Donner Photography at melissadonnerphotography.com.*

Harrisburg to be used as a bus shop. After some time, the building was torn down and a new bus shop was built. It was during this time that a piece of cardboard was found stashed in the wall. A virtual Whitehall School time capsule, the cardboard had a note, written in pencil, which I will include here as written:

> *This school house was built in the Year of June 21st 1939*
> *Mr. Ralph Maulkey*
> *earl Arkansas*
> *was boss*
> *His carpenters was Joe Minton*
> *Ray Gasaway*
> *Rex Bailey*
> *Roy Edwards*
> *3 men from earl Arkansas*
> *We DiD tHe Best*
> *We could.*
> *This was wrote on the Morning of 19th June 5:30 oc 1939*
> *Rex Bailey*
> *White Hall*
> *Arkansas*

More donations and unique finds began to surface. Mr. Ricky Parker of Cherry Valley donated an old Sears, Roebuck and Co. Number 4 bell for use in the bell tower. He dug it out of the St. Francis River, and no one knows how it got there or where it came from. The bell dates to 1886. Weiner Catholic School donated the chalkboard, and Mrs. Thelma Barr and Mr. Jimmy Foust each donated desks that came out of the old Whitehall School. Gene Crouch of Harrisburg donated an old coal-burning stove that came out of the old Hollender Shoe Shop in Harrisburg. It still works and heats the school on cold field trip days.

Perhaps one of Teressa's favorite donations to the school is a collection of poems from a 1928 autograph book belonging to Rachel Clampit Brown, who attended the Whitehall school as a child. At first, Rachel was hesitant to let Teressa use the poems, as they were personally written for her, and she didn't want to betray anyone's confidences. But Teressa assured Rachel that she was just interested in the poems and not in who wrote them and wouldn't put down any names. So Rachel relented. Here are a few of the best:

Coal-burning stove donated by Gene Crouch with American flag backdrop at E. Sloan Heritage School. *Photography by Melissa Donner Photography at melissadonnerphotography.com.*

What shall I write?
What shall it be?
Just two little words:
Remember me.

Roses are red;
Their stems are green;
Boys are cute,
But, oh, how mean.

Crackers are dry
Without any cheese,
So is a kiss
Without a squeeze.

Long may you live;
Short may you tarry;
Love who you may,
But mind who you marry.

Treasures like those are hard to come by for sure. When you visit, be sure to look for these poems and many more that Teressa has laminated.

During construction of the school, the Parkers found several old school remnants. The Homestead sits on the grounds where the old Whitehall school once sat, and therefore, items such as ink bottles and pieces of desk were unearthed during construction. Phil remembers that Cy and his friend Travis Easterling set the logs for the school in one day—no small feat when they were setting them all by hand at that time. Originally a two-room house, it was converted into the one-room schoolhouse for Homestead purposes, and leftover logs were turned into benches for students to sit on inside. The old seesaws from Harrisburg elementary are sitting out front.

It was almost like the school was meant to be there. And so it was no big surprise that students of the old Whitehall School wanted to come out and have a school reunion. Phil's father, Bobby, attended the Whitehall School and was prominent in the reunion planning. Tommye Rosa told me that she attended the reunion (though she had not attended the school) and heard former students talking about taking biscuits and ham for lunch. She also overheard one student say he opened his lunch pail to find a handful of walnuts and a hammer! Times were definitely different back then.

The E. Sloan Heritage School. *Parker Family Collection.*

My Papaw attended school just a few miles away at Wiley Crossing. I remember him telling me about taking a cold biscuit for his lunch and how that was all they had. He was embarrassed by this, and not wanting other children to see that was all he had, he would run off and sit under a tree by himself each day for lunch. One day, a friend of Papaw's offered to trade lunches sight unseen. He took the boy's lunch and ran as fast as he could with it before the boy realized his grave mistake. Papaw got to his tree and ripped the lid off the lunch pail to find a cold biscuit.

I guess the moral of that story was that Papaw's family was poor, sure, but so was everyone else living around here. When I was younger, I asked my other grandmother, Mary Sue Redd, why there weren't a lot of historical markers in and around Poinsett County. She said, "Honey, it's because we come from poor stock." I agreed, but the explanation never sat well with me. I thought then, and still think now, that our ancestors who worked to clear the land and fought to send their kids to school—even if it was only for a year or two—are who built this state, and that is something to be celebrated. I am very proud that the Homestead has chosen, in a way, to celebrate these regular folks.

One of my favorite parts of Homestead field trips is when it is lunchtime. To see hundreds of kids sprawled out on blankets enjoying a picnic on a nice fall day is heartwarming. Today, most students enjoy a sandwich for lunch, but when the old Whitehall school was up and running, lunch was a little bit different.

Red Williams told Phil that the "cool kids" in Whitehall took a pork chop sandwich on a biscuit for lunch and carried it in a Rex Jelly bucket. When Red graduated eighth grade and went to Harrisburg for high school, he carried his pork chop sandwich and Rex Jelly bucket to lunch with him to show he was cool. Well, the Harrisburg kids laughed and called him a hick. Poor old Red came home crying.

Mr. Williams learned that day that, unfortunately, what is cool in Whitehall isn't necessarily so elsewhere—a lesson my kids know all too well. But here at the Homestead, we are very proud of what is cool in Whitehall—so much so that a couple Christmases ago Teressa got Phil an old Rex Jelly bucket!

15

THE JOHNSON HOUSE, WAY STATION, BRUSH ARBOR AND COVERED BRIDGE

The Johnson House came to us one year with a field trip. Well, it didn't so much show up on a field trip, but its owner was a schoolteacher who attended field trips with his students and then contacted Teressa about a cabin he had in his backyard.

Mr. Johnson lived north of Jonesboro and the cabin that sat in his backyard belonged to his wife's family. I believe they used to live in it, and over time, as often happens, a newer house was built on their land. But for some reason, they left the cabin standing. Mr. Johnson said it was mostly being used as a tool shed and storage building and that he would love for the Homestead to have it.

Cy remembered going to tear it down, and so did I. My goodness, it was a hot day. Cy says that was the hottest day on which he has ever torn down a cabin. Cy, Roger Leder, Nick Martinez and Steve Marsh all helped to tear it down, but there was one caveat—Mr. Johnson wanted them to leave the floor. He was interested in building a shop where the cabin stood, so he wanted them to leave the base intact.

I remember going around the cabin and nailing jar lids on the logs to mark where they would go. Cabin logs are a little more difficult to lift and place than Lincoln logs, so you want to be sure you only have to lift and set a log once. There were a lot of windows and doors, plus a fireplace and many other things to number around, and it was a difficult job to figure out. But numbering was not nearly as difficult as what the boys were doing in a small backyard with a house in proximity. Because of the tight quarters, there was no way to get

A musician set up on the Johnson House porch—notice the jar lids nailed to the logs. *Photography by Melissa Donner Photography at melissadonnerphotography.com.*

The Johnson House. *Parker Family Collection.*

Cy's truck and a chain back there to pull the logs down. The boys worked all day chiseling out the concrete and then pulling down the logs one by one with crowbars. It was an awful, laborious, dirty, miserable day.

After they had gotten almost all of the logs loaded onto the trail and were cleaning up the rest of the yard, Mr. Johnson came out and told Cy that his wife was wanting to know why they were leaving the floor. Mr. Johnson told her, and she did not approve of his idea to leave it in the yard. So Mr. Johnson came out to tell Cy that his wife said the floor had to go as well. If they had known that earlier in the day it might not have been such an issue, but because of their trouble, the heat and just the sheer physical exertion of carrying all of those logs, Cy and crew cut up the floor into pieces with a chainsaw (which was the quickest way to get it out) then took it home and burned it.

Once brought back to the Homestead, the Johnson House was put up right across the old road from the way station and on the way to the covered bridge. Reconstructed in full, the Johnson House turned out to be quite comfy. The fireplace is gorgeous on the inside and does a wonderful job of heating the building. There are some cracks that used to make it a bit breezy in super cold weather, so Cy installed a floor heater, and it is now nice and cozy in there. It boasts a single room, with a full-sized poster bed and a rocking chair or two in front of the fireplace. There is also a table and a few shelves full of treasures, one of which is a family picture that belonged to Charlotte Mayberry Rushing. It is a picture of her father and brother standing with the first cotton picker to be purchased and brought into Poinsett County.

The large porch is a popular spot and has hosted many a weary traveler in its rockers. The Johnson House porch has even served as a stage for a rock band booked for a wedding. The Johnson House is one of the three "bed-and-breakfast cabins" as it does have a bed and fireplace, and there are plans to put in a bathroom.

Right across the street from the Johnson House is the way station, one of the three buildings put together using the logs from the old American Legion Hut in Trumann. A way station was a resting spot, somewhere you stopped on your way to somewhere else. They were often used as stops along a rail line, but at the Homestead we have set ours up as the first stop as you come over the bridge.

Inside, there are several unique treasures and artifacts. The old display case, which houses farm ledgers and other business papers, came out of the old Halk store in Cherry Valley. Also from the Halk store you will see a couple caskets, one of which is child sized, and a cooling board, which people used to be laid out on after they died. On the porch is an old paper cutter, and there are hopes to eventually build a printing and press shop that is separate from the post office to house the cutter and all the printing memorabilia. But until that time, the paper cutter greets visitors on the way station porch.

Also on the outside of the way station you will see the old steam whistle from the old Whitehall sawmill. And before you ask, yes, it is very loud.

Out in front of the way station is a beautiful brush arbor. Years ago, Mr. Hollan from Wynne had contacted us about the plantation bell that sits out in front of the barn. While at his house, we were immediately drawn to his beautiful and simply landscaped yard, full of monkey grass–lined paths and a focal-point brush arbor covered with wisteria. Teressa had been telling the boys for a couple years that she wanted an arbor, but all her requests fell on deaf ears—until they saw Mr. Hollan's. The men loved it as much as Teressa did, and the brush arbor you see at the Homestead is based on the beautiful one in the Hollan's backyard.

In front of the arbor is a heritage herb garden. It is beautiful when blooming in the spring and is one of the stops at our School Kids event. Students can learn about herbal remedies and also beekeeping there. On the north side of the garden, there is a colorful bottle tree—a staple in the South to keep the haints at bay. There is also a large piece of petrified wood and several unique and reclaimed decorative implements. But the focal point of the herb garden is a beautiful fountain that Teressa bought in my hometown of Fredericksburg, Texas.

Many a wedding is held under or in front of the arbor with the fountain as the backdrop. Another use of the arbor is as a shady resting spot while waiting in line for a wagon ride at the festival. It is a beautiful and unique addition to the Homestead, and we are very proud of it.

Leaving the arbor and rounding the corner between the way station and Johnson House, the road starts to go downhill, meandering toward the creek. There, you will find Parker's Bridge, a covered bridge connecting the Homestead to the old military road, which was the original road into Whitehall. Phil and Teressa started wanting a covered bridge and knew one of the best places to go and look at them was Amish country. But the expenses to get up there while putting Cy through college proved to be cost prohibitive, so they just decided to wait on it.

Then, fate intervened yet again. While at the airport waiting on their flight to watch Cy play football in El Paso, Texas, the airline made an

The Homestead brush arbor and heritage herb garden. *Parker Family Collection.*

announcement that they had overbooked. They were willing to let people rebook on a later flight and receive two round-trip tickets to another destination for free. Well, since booking on the later flight did not mean they would miss Cy's game, Phil and Teressa jumped on it and then had their free flights to Lancaster County, Pennsylvania.

While there, Phil says they looked at several bridges to get ideas. The Homestead bridge incorporates some of the Amish traditions. You will notice on the front there is a Pennsylvania Dutch Hex symbol, which stands for abundance in barn, field and home, and the larger sign in front of the bridge details Amish bridge traditions.

As far as constructing the bridge itself, the steel parts which the bridge sits on are from the old drive on the cotton scales out of the Whitehall gin, donated by Carl Woodham. These thirty-two-foot I-beams were loaded onto a sixteen-foot trailer and taken across the highway to the Homestead with a backhoe following the trailer and holding up the ends of the beams. The bridge timbers came out of the Poinsett County landfill and were there because another county bridge had been replaced. If you look on the interior

The covered bridge on a beautiful winter day. *Parker Family Collection.*

walls of the bridge, you will see several carved initials of Parkers, family and friends; feel free to add yours too.

The covered bridge was immediately a popular addition to the festival because the wagon rides could now cross the bridge and make a left onto the old military road, offering a scenic trip with Gary Brown's farm pastures to the right and the Homestead creek to the left. Many wagon riders love to wave to people who are congregating in the picnic area at Roberts Chapel as soon as they pass, and if you are working down there selling beans you can quickly wear your arm out waving at load after load of happy wagon riders.

And while enjoying the wagon rides visitors may hear some terminology they are unfamiliar with. Here at Homestead, we have a failsafe tip for inexperienced wagon riders that should clear up confusion about which direction "gee" and "haw" mean while working horses and mules. Just remember what James Holmes always says, "Gee means right, as in, 'Gee honey, you're right!'"

16

BEE BRANCH AND TONY'S 'TIQUES

The Bee Branch Cabin was one that came to the Homestead in a strange and interesting way. While Cy was attending the University of Central Arkansas in Conway, he had a professor reach out to him. The professor, who didn't have Cy in any of his classes, had just heard about the Homestead and that Cy was attending UCA.

This geography professor had assigned a particular project to his students that he thought would be of interest to Cy. The project assigned areas to students to go out and find old structures (like log cabins) and to diagram them and find out exactly where they were. He gave Cy a huge manila folder (one that he still has today) full of locations of cabins in the western part of the state, and Cy was very happy to have it.

For several months, if Cy had down time he would load up after class or after football practice and head out on the hunt with a road map, his manila folder and a friend, if he were lucky. If you ask Cy about the manila folder or, more specifically, about the students who turned in some of the reports in the manila folder, he will have some pointed opinions to share with you. He is convinced that some of those students were out and out liars, placing cabins in the middle of nowhere knowing that their teacher would not check them. Unfortunately for Cy, he tried to find them and was on a serious goose chase several times, crossing fences into pastures in the middle of nowhere and finding nothing.

On one occasion, the manila folder held a report with a picture of a huge two-story cabin with big logs and in good condition located near Bee Branch,

Arkansas. Cy was very interested to go and look at it and found it right where the student had said it would be. The only problem was that it had been burned to the ground two days before Cy got there. It was still smoldering. Cy was devastated, and the owners told him they were sorry it was just old and in the way and they didn't figure anyone would want it.

Already in the area, he decided to look for other cabins around Bee Branch, and that led him to two more, one of which is the Bee Branch mentioned in this chapter and the other which is currently stacked up "in the dry," as we call it, under the pole barn. There are several cabins or pieces of cabins stored there for future purposes, known or unknown.

Roger Leder, one of Cy's good college buddies, remembered getting those two cabins fondly. "Cy and I started to look at maps and explore the local areas for those hidden treasures. We found an old building up north of Conway, somewhere around the town of Bee Branch. This building was in decent shape and had some of the biggest logs I had ever seen."

It took Cy some time to find the owner of the building, as she no longer lived in the area. After asking several neighbors, he finally got a name of the building, the old Kincaid Place. He also got a name and phone number of Mrs. Barbara Morris from the Little Rock area, who now owned the land and cabin. She politely informed Cy that she had no intention of getting rid of the cabin but did speak to him at length about the Homestead. She thought the project was worthwhile but didn't want to give up her cabin.

Cy ended the call cordially and proceeded to call her back every couple months to check in and ask for it again. After a few calls, he gave up and decided to quit bothering her. And wouldn't you know it, that was when she called him. Mrs. Morris said that there had been vandalism on her property, people ripping tin off and shooting out the windows. She told Cy she wanted him to have it, and he immediately enlisted Roger to help him go and get it.

According to Roger, "We loaded up one afternoon after our classes were out for the day and took off to get the building. We had to pass through a small town called Greenbrier that was a known speed trap. The speed limit through town was forty-five miles per hour. I think we were doing a little over fifty when we noticed the cop pulling out with his blue lights on. I will never forget when the officer walked up to the truck and started making small talk and asking questions. Cy told the officer that we were kind of in a hurry, and so if he was going to give us a ticket, then go ahead and do it because we had to go. The officer walked back to his car and came back with the ticket and told us to have a nice day."

The Homestead grandkids take sledding seriously. (From left to right) Caroline, Kaiser and Kyra on a draft sled, Bee Branch in the background. *Parker Family Collection.*

I was not surprised at all to hear Roger's story about my husband's impatience. The rest of Roger's story about getting the cabin goes smoothly and without intervention by local law enforcement. "We arrived at the location and started by numbering each log on the building with Mason jar lids, which we wrote numbers on and nailed to the logs. This was so we would know which log was which and where it needed to go when we started to put it back up at the Homestead. Then we started to tear the building down one log at a time. We did not have a tractor or any type of loader to put the logs on the trailer—he and I loaded the logs up one by one. We must have been in a lot better shape than we are now because even though it was hard, we somehow managed to get the logs loaded. We went back to Conway and, the next day, took the trailer load of logs to the Homestead to reconstruct the building."

Cy, Roger and Steve Marsh put the cabin back up the next day. The Bee Branch was originally a two-story cabin, but once the boys got it home and set, the top part was leaning pretty seriously toward the south. Cy and Phil made

> ## Glazed Almond Cookies
>
> Here is a recipe for one of my favorite holiday treats, glazed almond cookies. Hope you enjoy them as much as we do!
>
> *Cookies*
> 1 cup butter, softened
> ¾ cup sugar
> 1 teaspoon almond extract
> 2 cups all-purpose flour
> ½ teaspoon baking powder
> ¼ teaspoon salt
>
> *Glaze*
> 1½ cups powdered sugar
> 1 teaspoon almond extract
> 4 to 5 teaspoons water
> Sliced almonds for garnish
>
> Heat oven to 400 degrees. Using a stand or electric mixer, combine all cookie ingredients in large bowl. Beat at medium speed, scraping bowl often, until well mixed. Drop dough by rounded teaspoonfuls onto ungreased cookie sheets 2 inches apart. Flatten balls to ¼-inch thick with bottom of buttered glass dipped in sugar. Bake seven to nine minutes or until edges are very lightly browned. Cool one minute on cookie sheet; remove to cooling rack. Cool completely. Combine all glaze ingredients except almonds in a small bowl with wire whisk. Decorate cooled cookies with glaze and sliced almonds as desired.

some adjustments to try to stabilize and straighten the building, but in the end, they decided the best thing to do would be to shorten it some. It is now a story and a half with a nice sized loft. The cabin features an awesome fireplace that stretches floor to ceiling on the inside. Phil brought home the rock for it from some stone leftover after a job. His boss Dicky Bradley donated the stone.

The Bee Branch is also the first (and so far the only) cabin for which Cy trimmed the inside with rope. You can see it in the corners and up around the ceiling, and it is beautiful. Upstairs, you will see some wrought-iron fencing closing in the loft. This came from our house. When we bought it from Mrs. Ruthie, she let us know that Mr. Johnny had some fencing and where it was and said she hoped we would like to use it someday.

A funny story about the Bee Branch is that Cy graduated college sometime after it was completed. For his first interview, Bradley Beetch came out to the Homestead to talk to Cy and get a feel for who he was. Cy walked him all over the place, taking

Homestead boys (left to right) Cy Parker, Roger Leder and Steve Marsh preparing to reconstruct the Bee Branch Cabin. *Parker Family Collection.*

Left: The Bee Branch Cabin. *Parker Family Collection.*

Below: Tony's 'Tiques. *Parker Family Collection.*

time to explain everything from the Homestead events to building techniques, and Brad took everything in. The finished up their tour by relaxing in some rocking chairs on the porch of the Bee Branch, where Brad looked at Cy and said, "So why do you want a job again?"

It is sometimes hard for us to see the forest for the trees, and as Parkers we don't always realize how magnificent the place looks to people on their first visit. It is pretty easy for people like Brad to think that we must have full-time employees and a steady (and substantial) income coming in from the Homestead. Brad was very surprised to hear from Cy that it is just the few of us that do all the routine maintenance at the place and that the Homestead is only open ten days a year. Brad did end up hiring Cy, and though he is no longer Cy's boss, the two are great friends. Cy still teases Brad about that day.

Be sure and notice a couple more things while you are here, such as Tony's 'Tiques and the back door that leads to nowhere. Tony's 'Tiques is the area to the north of the Bee Branch where there is a fence, some implements on display and some old saw blades with mysterious faces on them. Tony was Teressa's brother who passed away in 2009. In his later years, nothing made him happier than scouring country roads in search of some "treasures" to bring to Teressa (whether she really wanted them or not). This area is full of some (but not all) of his finds, and we love to look at the saw blades and remember Tony fondly. As for the door, if you were to open the back door of the Bee Branch, you would see that it opens up to nothing but a bunch of woods. There have been conversations since the Bee Branch was built to add on a kitchen and bathroom out that back door, but you know what they say about the best-laid plans. We do have the majority of items we need to fill the kitchen and restroom once they are built, and I still hold out hope that sometime in the near future construction will begin.

See, I have more of a vested interest in the kitchen and bathroom than most because the Bee Branch cabin is where my family sets up each year on Christmas Eve to wait for Santa. At the Homestead, Santa doesn't come to our houses, he visits the cabins. Phil and Teressa wait on Santa in the Foust House while my niece Kyra and her dad, David Burns, wait on him to visit the Johnson House. We are always sure to let the fire die down just enough so Santa can get in and out of the cabins without getting singed, and in the morning, a big bunch of extended family come over for breakfast, to exchange gifts and to watch the kids play over at the Foust House. But it can be a long night sleeping in the Bee Branch without a restroom. Luckily, all we have to do is run across the field in the cold to use the public restrooms, and I guess in a way that is a pioneer experience in itself.

In recent years, Cy and I have ventured into some new Parker Homestead territory, by hosting a Valentine's Day Dinner and a wine tasting. The Bee Branch is prominently featured in both events, as it is a pretty good size and has the bed upstairs and a futon bed downstairs for people who wish to stay overnight. During the wine tasting, the Bee Branch is always used as the dessert cabin and has a varying menu of fudges, truffles, cookies, toffee and more.

17

THE FOUST HOUSE

The Foust House—or the Two Story, as we call it—was the first building I ever went to tear down with Cy. Talk about an experience. We pulled up to the deserted and dilapidated cabin, and by all appearances, it was a total disaster. I couldn't believe we were there and wasting our time. My cousin Celia Deckelman was with us, and I can tell you she felt the same way. Cy told me later that even Phil thought it was a complete waste of time to go and get it.

Cy was not the least bit deterred. He got out of the truck and began systematically wrapping a chain around logs, one at a time, starting on the top, and then attached the chain to the truck. Celia and I loaded back up too, and at once, Cy lurched the truck forward, ripping the logs down. Having never been on the real working end of a truck, I can tell you it was quite a shock. I thought the whole axle would be ripped out from under us. My limited experience in helping my daddy pull a boat up a ramp at the lake or even using Dad's truck to hoist a deer up to field dress had felt nothing like that.

Cy loaded up all the logs and also managed to salvage the original staircase from the cabin. Once home, I remember Cy and Phil looking the logs over and realizing that several of the logs on the front side were rotten and would have to be replaced. Aesthetically, to use some newly milled logs on the front would just not look right, so Phil and Cy decided to move logs from the middle wall to replace the rotten logs on the front. Inside the cabin, you will notice the new milled logs on the middle wall. They came from Jim May's sawmill in Birdeye. You can see where the boys tried to make them look

Cy Parker rocking on the porch of the Foust House. *Parker Family Collection.*

hand hewed the best they could. Even though they were able to move some of the middle logs to the front, one log on the outside facing the schoolhouse still had to be replaced with a newly milled log. It was custom cut and measures four inches thick, twelve inches tall and twenty-eight inches long.

Additionally, the original floor joists on the bottom floor were too rotted to use and had to be replaced with milled lumber. The original joists were salvaged though. We cut them up and used them as the posts on the porches.

Once the replacements were milled, it was time to set the logs and stand the Foust House up once more, which was a feat in itself—one of super balance and concentration. The bottom logs were all set by hand, with Cy, Steve Marsh, Roger Leder, Nathan Thomas and Nick Martinez helping. Once the first floor was up, the original second-floor joists were set. They had to be flipped upside down to use because they were sagging really badly. But once flipped over, they were just fine. Then came the feats of balance.

The boys laid boards across the upstairs joists, which were very springy, and stood there waiting for Phil to lift and swing one log at a time to them with a SkyTrac. The Foust House was the first cabin that logs were set this way at the Homestead, and although the SkyTrac made the lifting a lot easier, it made the builders quite wary. Anyone who has ever rocked on the front porch of the Foust House will be able to testify to the awesome and perpetual breeze that comes across the field. Windy conditions combined with

The Foust House. *Parker Family Collection.*

a SkyTrac with brakes that were shot but swinging logs weighing hundreds of pounds at boys balanced on skinny boards made the construction a tense time for everyone. I remember Nathan Thomas saying his father warned him to be extra careful because Phil Parker had always been accident prone and they were gonna be up pretty high.

Despite the high-wire act, the logs were all set, and the cabin looked remarkably well—nothing at all like the building Celia and I had gone to tear down with Cy. After it was put up, it was time to start preparing the inside. Nick Martinez had a unique experience at this stage of the project. When Nick came in one weekend to work on the Foust House, Teressa asked him if he could pull all the nails off the inside of the logs. He said sure and that it shouldn't take him more than an hour or two. Nick pulled nails all weekend and still didn't get finished.

The Foust House has a front living area, a kitchen area and an upstairs bedroom. It has a wraparound porch across the front and the east sides. The back of the east side of the porch was enclosed to make a bathroom, which features a pull-chain water closet, a claw foot tub, a pedestal sink and a mirror framed by a wagon wheel. The tub was Teressa's, and she had used it in her classroom at school filled with pillows as a good-behavior reading nook. After she retired, it ended up as the goat's favorite high spot in Julie Bell's pen before being reconditioned and put in the Foust House. The toilet came from Mr. John Ellis of Jonesboro, and there's a great but unprintable story about the acquisition of it. If you have a sordid sense of humor and do not easily offend, feel free to ask us.

The kitchen area is decorated with a table that came out of the old Halk store in Cherry Valley and a tobacco basket that came from there as well. The lights are made out of lanterns Phil converted, and there is an old farm sink. The stove and oven really work and are cooked on several times a year. Cy built the cabinets. Even the trashcan has history—it is a flower barrel that came from a store owned by Miss Elizabeth's father, Sam Clements.

Above the kitchen door you might notice a huge beam that is set up as a shelf. Teressa had a unique story about how that got there. She said she was busy helping some people with a wedding and knew she hadn't seen Cy all day, but she didn't know what he was up to. She said toward the end of the day, an extremely dirty and tired Cy showed up around the church and told her that he had put the beam up in the kitchen—by himself. It sits above the doorframe, so about seven feet in the air. The beam measures six by fifteen inches and is fourteen or fifteen feet long. Teressa said she has no idea how in the world he set that himself without a hoist or pulley or anything. Cy says he was in a lot better shape then. Even so, it is a pretty impressive feat of strength.

In the living room, please notice the original staircase. The steps get steeper as you go up, and we always warn people to duck and watch their heads. There are antique lamps, rockers and other items to look at in the living area, which is finished out with a couch and a table and chairs.

The fireplace is gorgeous, and most everyone that comes into the Foust House is sure to notice and comment on it. There are a couple funny stories about its origins. Phil, Teressa and I took Caroline to see the Disney movie *Monsters Inc.* in 2001, which was right after the Foust House logs had been set. Of course, Caroline and I are watching the movie intently while Phil and Teressa are busy noticing the fireplace of the main character, Sully. They both loved it, and Phil thought the little girl in the movie favored Caroline, so he came home and built a replica of Sully's fireplace in the Foust House fireplace for her.

Another fireplace story is that around the same time, Cy was tearing down a cabin somewhere around Russellville. It had a large chimney on it, but he

Teressa's ancestors in front of a cabin that looks very similar to the Foust House. *Parker Family Collection.*

did not want to bring the rock home, just the logs. Phil insisted he bring the rock, and Cy was adamantly against it. He thought the rocks were ugly and that Phil wouldn't be able to make anything that looked good out of them. Well, the beautiful Foust House Fireplace (as well as the fireplace in Johnson House) came from that load of ugly rock. Phil is an artist.

Finishing out the living room is a large picture of Grandpa Shearer, Teressa's great-great-great-grandpa. There is also a small picture of him in the bathroom that you should pay close attention to. Upon completion of the Foust House, Teressa found an old photo at the home of Wilma and Freda Heeb. They were Teressa's great-aunts, sisters who never married and still lived in their parents' home. The photo (the one now in the bathroom of the Foust House) is of Teressa's great-great-great-grandparents with their son-in-law, John Martin Heeb, who is Teressa's great-great-grandfather.

What is so striking about the photo is that the three of them are sitting on the porch on the side of the log house they lived in, which looks eerily like the Foust House. If you wrapped the porch around the side, they would almost be identical. There is an upstairs window clearly visible in the same spot of one of our windows upstairs. Also in the picture is a trunk sitting on their front porch. Teressa now has that trunk, the one that her great-great-grandpa John Heeb brought all his worldly possessions to America in when he moved from Switzerland in 1941.

Going upstairs (watch your head), be sure to notice the size of the furniture in relation to the narrow staircase. There was no way to get any furniture up those stairs, so we had to leave one of the outside gables open to swing the furniture in. Once everything was in, the gable was sealed up, so everything that is up there is up there to stay.

Because the Foust House was the first cabin that was going to be set up for people to stay in, Teressa was worried about finding iron beds. Phil dismissed her worries and famously said, "You can get those anywhere, anytime for fifty dollars." After searching far and wide and not finding anything that would work, the beds you could find anywhere finally turned up in Lonoke. Suffice it to say that they weren't fifty dollars.

The Foust House has many uses: bed-and-breakfast cabin, a stop on the holidays wine tasting event and Phil and Teressa's base of operations during Christmas season when the kids are all out of school. But when it was first built, Mark Holmes claimed it for himself.

Mark was Parker Homestead's very first (and self-proclaimed) mayor, and no one argued with him. Mark volunteered innumerable hours at the Homestead, and he loved to rock on the front porch and tell people it was his cabin. We have missed him terribly since he moved, but he is always sure to check in when he comes back to visit family.

A few years back and during an exceptionally cold night, Cy, Caroline and I decided to stay in the Foust House for the night. It is just something that's fun to do as a mini getaway sometimes, even if it is just in our backyard. When we were preparing to go out to the cabin for the night, my friend Travis Eddleman showed up, so we just took him out there to spend the night with us. Travis and Cy loaded the fireplace up as full as they could possibly get it before we went upstairs to bed as it was supposed to be in the twenties that night. We all slept wonderfully.

Sometime the next morning we were awakened by Phil making an awful racket downstairs. We ran down to see what was going on and found Phil ripping up the floor under the hearth! Cy's friend Steve Marsh had shown up that morning as well and was watching the catastrophe unfold. Cy yelled at Phil to stop, but Phil said the building was on fire. Sure enough, the floor was smoking, and Phil, Cy and Travis all went outside to get another look. Cy said the floor just got hot but was not on fire, but Phil insisted and even thought about taking a chainsaw to the floor.

Things escalated quickly, and Teressa (who was holding Caroline because she was scared to death with all the commotion about a fire) agreed with Cy that there wasn't any danger of a fire; the floor was just hot. Cy said something like, "If Dad comes back in here with a chainsaw, I am just gonna have to lay him out." Fortunately for everyone involved, Phil did not come back in with a chainsaw, and the area of floor that he ripped up has been covered. I can tell you that one good thing came out of this incident: Cy and Travis are very careful about overfilling the fireplace now.

18

PARKER HOMESTEAD HONORABLE MENTION

The Bacon Hotel

Though not technically on the grounds of the Homestead, the first and last historic building you will see on Homestead Road is the Bacon Hotel. Listed on the National Register of Historic Places, the Bacon Hotel is owned by Cy and me. The following information about the Bacon Hotel has been generously provided by the Poinsett County Historical Society.

The two-story structure, which is painted yellow and boasts eight rooms, sits on the south side of Homestead Road and dates to the time when the new little town of White Hall was first being plotted. Mr. E.A. Gilbert purchased the NE ¼, SE ¼ Section 23, T10N, R03W and laid out Gilbert's Division in White Hall "as shown in plat filed for record May 17, 1912," according to the society's records. The Bacon Hotel is located on the former Lot 4, Block 4 of Gilbert's Division facing the now bygone Front Street that ran parallel to the railroad tracks.

This tract was purchased on May 28, 1922, by James William Bacon for the "consideration of $100.00 paid." Although the date carved in the steps beside the front porch of the hotel is only two days after the transaction date, Bacon, who was a carpenter, did construct the hotel according to Dorothy Bacon, a granddaughter-in-law, and other descendants. On August 9, 1912, Bacon and his wife, Mary Elizabeth Patterson Bacon, took out a mortgage for the "principal sum of $750.00 with 8% interest from date due one year after date."

The raison d'être for the Bacon Hotel was apparently to provide lodging for the many timber company officials who would travel to Whitehall on business and for the "drummers" or traveling salesmen. Mr. John E.

> ### Haunted Hotel?
>
> Over the years, Phil and Teressa (and now Cy and I) have received many questions about whether or not the Bacon Hotel is haunted. Though I have done my best to discount this type of talk, the rumors persist of strange goings on and even a murder, though there is no evidence supporting any of these claims. Despite my best efforts, area ghost hunters have asked many times to investigate for themselves.
>
> The only story I have that might be spooky regarding the hotel is the persistent (yet inconsistent) story about a horrific injury and treatment at the hotel. It seems that either a black man who was dragged by a mule or a white man who was hit by a train was disemboweled. Whichever man it was, he lived through the initial trauma and was rushed to the hotel, where Dr. Chambers treated them. According to local legend, Dr. Chambers completely removed the injured man's entrails, hand washed them in a washtub and then put them back. The best part of this outlandish story is that the man supposedly lived to tell the tale.
>
> Despite the fact that the accidents and men described are different, in both stories, the remedy and doctor are the same. Several old-time Whitehall residents relay the story as the gospel truth. Mr. Johnny said he had never heard that story before but that there was a Mr. Chambers who at one time resided in the Bacon Hotel, and his brother was in fact a doctor. Spooky, sure, but no death, no murder and no haunting as far as I know, and Cy and I own the building.

Roberts, owner of the Bacon Hotel for many years, stated that many lumber executives from up north would come stay in the hotel while checking on their business interests in and around the Whitehall area and the going rate was one dollar per day.

According to Edward Maddox of Harrisburg, the Bacon Hotel was also used by a land agent named Propes who would travel to Wisconsin to solicit German and Swiss immigrants to visit Arkansas. Propes was selling L'Anguile river-bottom land for as much as fifty dollars an acre (compared to the going rate of fifteen to twenty dollars an acre) and was bringing the visitors to

Whitehall only during the dry season when the river was more subdued. The relatively secluded Bacon Hotel proved a perfect location, for it kept the immigrants from socializing in the more populous Harrisburg where they might find out they were being swindled. At least one Swiss immigrant family's descendants still reside in Poinsett County, although a connection with Mr. Propes is unknown.

Locals called it "the Sunrise Hotel" because of the beautiful wooden sunburst in the gable facing today's Highway 1. But unfortunately, much like many of the other businesses in the bustling new town of Whitehall, the Bacon Hotel was a relatively short-lived venture. Longtime Whitehall resident Mrs. Fanny Brown was married in 1914 and said that at the time of her marriage, the Bacon Hotel was no longer in use as a hotel. She did remember the Bacon family living there at one time, but she stated that she did not know them well because "they were too hifalutin" for her.

Agreeing with her recollections, county records state that on June 5, 1913, Bacon sold the property. It is not clear whether Bacon was unable to pay the mortgage or simply decided to sell. The property was then sold back to Mr. E.A. Gilbert in 1914 with three more transactions until the Roberts family purchased the Bacon Hotel and the surrounding properties in 1919.

By this time, the forests were largely cut over and the stump-strewn land was being cleared for agricultural use. Consequently, the economic boom associated with such towns naturally subsided, and this might have been the contributing factor in the demise of the Bacon Hotel as a boarding house. William D. Roberts and his sons—W.S., J.E. (or Mr. Johnny as we called him) and James—owned the Roberts Cotton Oil Company in Memphis, Tennessee. They subsequently petitioned to convert the platted town back into farm acreage and peach orchard. Thereafter, the Bacon Hotel was utilized as a residence for the Roberts's farm managers and their families.

Chambers was the first manager and stayed at the hotel into the 1920s. He was followed by Joe Dowdy, who was farm manager until 1930. Mrs. Ellen Fair, the lady who sold Phil her Home Comfort stove, remembered Mr. Dowdy living in the hotel. She said her brothers would wrestle to see who would earn the privilege of opening the livestock gate leading to Mr. Dowdy's house, as at that time, all animals were free range and the railroad had to have a fence up against it to keep animals off the tracks.

After Mr. Dowdy's time as farm manager ended, the Hall family resided at the Bacon Hotel through 1937. Dorothy Jean Hall Bellinger remembered having electricity during their years at the hotel, and Mr. Johnny told Teressa that he put electricity in around 1936, though indoor plumbing came later.

Haunted Homestead?

Speaking of hauntings, one year while getting ready for Haunted Homestead, Teressa and her cousin Vickie were out in the barn working long after everyone else had gone to sleep. They went out to get started at about 10:00 p.m. on a week night, causing Phil to remark, "You Heeb women have more stamina than anybody I know." (Both Teressa and Vickie's maiden names were Heeb.) Well, out back in the barn late at night is always kind of spooky, especially around Halloween, but with the two of them together they weren't afraid.

Sometime after midnight, they sat down on a bench in front of the old herb garden, facing the barn, to admire their handiwork and rest a minute. All at once, a loud knocking came from the barn. Teressa and Vickie looked at each other and exclaimed at the same time, "What was that?" They listened for another moment together but it was quiet. Just when they decided it was nothing, the knocking started up again.

Well, being who they were, they decided they had to investigate. Vickie pulled out the trusty pocketknife her dad, Shorty Heeb, had given her, grabbed ahold of Teressa and said "Let's check it out." They hopped on the Kawasaki mule and slowly approached the barn. Again, it was quiet. They circled the barn, all the while trying to convince one another it was nothing. They spooked a little more when they were startled by large figures hanging from ropes inside the barn before realizing they were just props for Haunted Homestead that were glowing white in the dark.

Vickie wanted to go in the barn and check it out, but Teressa refused. So Vickie held her knife out in front of her and crept up on the props while Teressa watched from the safety of the open doorway. Vickie poked around at all the props. But nothing was there, and it was still quiet inside. She came back out, but the pair was too freaked out at this point to continue anything else outside that night. As they started to leave, the knocking started up again so they jumped in the mule to high-tail it up to Phil and Teressa's house. As they came around the side of the barn, the knocking got even louder, and all at once Teressa realized what the sound was. There was a rabbit hutch under the lean-to of the barn, and one of the rabbits was in there thumping his foot.

It took them a while to decide whether or not to even tell anyone how scared they had gotten, but it does make for a wonderful Homestead moment.

Mrs. Bellinger also remembers that when she lived in the Bacon Hotel it was painted white.

One funny story relayed by Mrs. Bellinger is that her father made a batch of peach brandy and had it stored in five-gallon kegs in the upstairs room on the east side of the hotel. She and her sister snuck up there and got themselves a drink or two and split a cigar. When they came back downstairs her mother was serving lunch to all the farmhands, and it was at that precise moment, and in front of everybody, that the girls lost their lunches. She said that was the only spanking she ever remembered getting from her father.

After the Halls moved out, Henry Crider and his family lived in the building up until about 1944. After that, Mr. Johnny assumed the role of farm manager but did not live at the hotel. Three more men who were working for Mr. Johnny (though not technically managers) lived at the hotel with their families in succession until the early 1960s.

Brenda Wessner Brimer pulled in my drive one hot day in July 2013 and got out of her car to look around at the hotel. This is not all that uncommon, and we have become accustomed to sharing it with people. I went to greet her and discovered that she lived in the hotel from 1955 or so until she graduated high school in 1961. She told me that the bathroom was put in her senior year and that the whole house was heated by the wood stove downstairs. She remembers having parties in the peach-packing shed (which is next door) and also told me that a quilt her mother made hangs in Roberts Chapel now.

No one has lived in the Bacon Hotel since Brenda's family moved out, though it has been used for various purposes. Mr. Johnny built the home Cy and I live in now, which sits across the yard from the hotel. He and his wife, Miss Elizabeth, lived there until they died. One funny story about Mr. Johnny, Miss Elizabeth and the hotel is that Miss Elizabeth did not believe in washing clothes inside the house; she said civilized and refined people used a wash house. So up until her death, they washed their clothes in "the big house" across the yard. After Miss Elizabeth passed away and Mr. Johnny married Mrs. Ruthie Roberts, she told him that she was not too keen on carting her laundry back and forth across the yard to the big house, and so he finally put a washer and dryer in the residence.

Mr. Johnny was pretty good at woodworking and refinished lots of pieces in the hotel over the years. He also used it for storage. The hotel was used as a polling center for Scott Township residents for many years, and I have had people on the Parker Homestead send me Facebook messages to say the first time they ever voted was at the Bacon Hotel.

A true local landmark, the Bacon Hotel is significant as the most visible link to the boom era and subsequent agricultural transformation of the historic community of Whitehall. The Bacon Hotel is also listed in the National Register of Historic Places as the best example of folk Victorian-style architecture in Poinsett County and as one of the better examples of a railroad-related hotel in the entire state.

19

THE OUTTAKES

There are many stories and artifacts that are not expressly addressed in this book for several reasons. Maybe there wasn't a good place to fit them in, or maybe they weren't associated with a particular cabin. At any rate, I would love to share a few of them with you here.

The Civil War Reeanactors, or Arkansas Seventh, have been coming to the Homestead for many years. Karl and Mary Kunkel were the leaders and were joined by many, many more enthusiastic soldiers, including Hawkeye, Jackie and more. Randy Jones owns the cannon that so many people love to see. At the festival, we shoot the cannon off on the hour, every hour. People who have been before are aware of this and will go over to watch. Unsuspecting visitors will jump out of their skins when the full complement of the cannon is unloaded.

A few years ago, one of our neighbors, Kim Wallace, who lives about a half mile away, was sitting at home enjoying her day when the cannon was fired off. She later told Tommye that she almost called 911 thinking a meth lab had blown up somewhere in the area. Then her husband, John, informed her, "No, it's just the Parkers' cannon. No big deal."

While I was attending Arkansas State, I had a class with Matthew Mooney. When he was in high school, he had worked at the Homestead several times doing things like loading sorghum trailers or helping to clean up before the festival. He told me about an instance when Phil had asked him and another young man, Justin Jones, to pick up and move some logs. They both grabbed their respective ends of a log and picked it up when Justin

The Homestead cannon, owned by Randy Jones. *Photography by Melissa Donner Photography at melissadonnerphotography.com.*

immediately dropped his and took off running like he was on fire. Matthew said he was pretty angry because the log was heavy and there he was, just holding one end, so he hollered at Justin—who had slowed some—"Where are you going?"

Justin screamed, "Snakes!" Matthew looked down to see that there was a bed of copperheads under his end of the log. He said he does not think he has ever dropped a log and run that fast in his life, and that is really saying something as Matthew and his whole family were always very talented athletes.

Over the years, Parker Homestead hosted many events that did not turn out to be annual affairs. One that Teressa really wanted to have was the Homestead Holidays living nativity. She enlisted the help of area churches, which were very excited to come out and participate, and all started well. I remember one year in particular that John and Amber Sutton played Joseph and Mary, and another year Butch and Krissy Sadler played them. Carl Steyer and Mark Sadler were Roman soldiers, and we had an assortment of angels, shepherds, farm animals and more.

But other years were not so great. There were the years that were bitter cold and none of the church volunteers, many of whom were elderly, were able to show up. Because of a couple of these types of years in a row (I believe one of them was smack in the middle of an ice storm), we discontinued the event. I remember parking cars one of those cold years—I was stationed up by the grain bins and far away from anyone to talk to, standing out in the snow. Just when I thought I might freeze to death, an unknown elderly couple returned to their car, and the sweet little lady offered me her cup of hot chocolate. I took it and gulped it down quickly, not caring in the slightest that she had already enjoyed half of it. Later that same night, Diana Davis returned to her vehicle, saw me shivering and gave me the pair of gloves off her warm hands.

Yet another living nativity disaster was when LaFarrell Wess's sheep got spooked somehow and ran off. LaFarrell was very worried and looked until well after dark, when he decided to just come back and try in the morning. I'm not sure now the string of events that led up to this incident, but all I know is Teressa came to get me because she saw a sheep. She snuck up on it and roped it, and the thing took off like it was a wild mustang. Teressa was being dragged like she was a rag doll, and I grabbed on to the rope to try to help her. It was about this time that the sheep bolted south, and Teressa fell down, letting go of the rope and screaming for me to hold on. And I held on buddy—around the corner of Julie Bell's barn and into the blacksmith shop where the sheep cut back at a very sharp angle and ran me right into the big anvil.

I'm here to tell you that homesteading is not for the faint of heart, nor is it for anyone with a weak constitution or a low pain threshold. I have never had a contusion like that before or since, and I don't plan to. And in case you are wondering, I didn't let go of the darn sheep.

Speaking of people who do not have weak constitutions, Steve Marsh, Roger Leder and Nick Martinez helped to build the entire back half of the Homestead while going to college with Cy. They showed up for work each Saturday morning at 7:00 a.m., and though they may have looked a little worse for wear after their late Friday nights, they got the job done and always managed to have a good time while doing it.

With all of the log cabins and wooden barns, fire is a real concern. We've had a few close calls, but none of them has caused any real damage. Here are some of our close calls with fire.

During Haunted Homestead, the first thing people see when they come through the gate is a Farmall Tractor spotlighted with a red light and running an old hay baler. It makes a terrible racket and would be really scary by itself, but to add insult to injury, there is also an old orchard heater full of burnt oil and diesel lit up and shooting a flame that will burn for several hours. It is quite the display.

One night, just as things were getting started, the flames leapt to the ground and caught the dry grass and hay on fire. Teressa was doing her walkthrough to make sure everything was running smoothly when she saw the fire. Teressa started screaming, "Fire!" at the top of her lungs, but no one paid any attention to her—they thought it was park of the show.

Unable to get anyone to listen to her or to find a water hose in the dark, Teressa ran out back, got a truck and headed for the bathrooms where she knew a couple water hoses were. She threw them in the back of the truck and barreled through the Homestead heading for the fire. Now this, people noticed. Workers started wondering why on earth there was a vehicle driving through in the dark with all the pedestrians about and paused to come and see who the person was who was driving.

When Teressa arrived back at the scene of the fire, she jumped out to grab the hoses but they weren't there. In her hurry and panic, she left the tailgate down, and they all flew out somewhere between the restrooms and the fire. All she could do at this point was to run in circles and scream for help.

But people were noticing. Phil emerged from the cemetery to see about the vehicle and then saw the flames from there. He yelled, "Fire!" and he, Carl Steyer and Randy Jones headed in that direction. On their way, they found the water hoses that had fallen out of the back of the truck.

Luckily, Mark Sadler was already on the scene and had grabbed a hose he knew about hidden down in the sorghum mill. The hose was not nearly long enough to reach, but he turned it on anyway and was able to hold the fire at bay by wetting the ground all around it until the other guys arrived. Once the hoses Teressa lost on the road were hooked up, the fire was put down with no real damage, except to Teressa's humor, who kept saying no one would listen to her.

One other Homestead fire story involves Teressa's aunt Helen Heeb. During trick or treat, Aunt Helen was sitting quietly at her daughter Vickie's table, which was set up in the picnic area beside Roberts Chapel. This was the same location where just a week before, Vickie and Annetta had inadvertently set the large hay fire. At any rate, Helen was sitting there at the table, and Vickie had gone up the hill for something. Vickie was at the top of the steps when she heard her mother say quietly, "The table's on fire down here. Hey Vick, the table's on fire, come here Vick and do something, the table's on fire." You would have to know Aunt Helen to fully understand her soft spoken, smooth and beautiful voice, which makes the story even funnier.

It seems that one of the candles on the table had fallen over and caught almost everything on the table on fire, melting several items. Once again, Vickie ran down there and beat the fire back with her trusty broom until someone brought water hoses to her aid.

My last outtake is a favorite Haunted Homestead story, one from Clark's Cabin. We were working up front that year, and the group coming through was a mixed group, including a family with children ages ten or so up to teenagers and two young couples who were not related to the family. Working that night up front was Cy, Seth and Mandy Whitmire, Nathan Thomas, Shane and Kaity Adams, Morgan Reddmann, me and Mitch Jones. Of course, we ran out and scared the tar out of the group, and Seth took things a step further by grabbing the ten-year-old girl, hoisting her up over his shoulder, and walking toward the woods with her.

I was unaware of where Seth was or what he was doing. I was just laughing and with Morgan and Kaity trying to round up the rest of the group to send them on to the next station. At that point, Mandy ran up to tell us that her husband was taking this child off. She whispered to me that the family, though unsuspecting of who Seth was because he was wearing a toe sack over his head, were close family friends of the Whitmires, so he was just having a little fun with them.

I started to holler at him, laughing and saying, "Seth! Bring the kid back! You can't have that one." The young couple (who was not related to the family that Seth was torturing) had made their way over to us and were laughing too, as we began to watch the scared mother beat Seth with her purse in a desperate attempt to get her child back. All at once, one of the people we rounded up said, "You know, we were in line with that nice family for three hours and had no idea they were part of the show!"

I looked at them blankly and calmly said, "They're not."

The couples turned right around, grabbed each other tighter, and one of the ladies burst into tears, saying, "I can't take this! They're going to kill us all!" And they headed back for the trailer to the parking lot.

Seth ripped off his toe sack and identified himself to the family, and they all had a good laugh. Over the years, we have not killed anyone at Haunted Homestead, and everyone has in fact made it out the gates they came in.

We have been so fortunate to entertain and educate all these years, and whether it has been by accident or design is of little consequence now. Parker Homestead has become a community institution, and I wrote this book as a way of giving back. My goal is that teachers and other visitors to Homestead can use this to learn even more about our history. I hope the friends who helped us along the way will enjoy reliving some of the stories shared here, the ones they remember and the ones they don't. I expect a bunch of people will enjoy some Cajun éttouffeé at home, and I also pray that Caroline, Kyra and Kaiser can look to this book in the future. Maybe it will be at a point in their lives when they may need a little encouragement. Because as they grow up, they will learn that things aren't always going to be easy, but I hope they come to see that the most worthwhile things in life almost never are.

I want the grandkids to read what their grandparents accomplished through good old-fashioned hard work and prayer. And maybe that day, the day they need a little encouragement, they will gain an understanding that this wonderful legacy of Parker Homestead passed down to them did not come easy. But if they choose to continue working hard, the legacy of Parker Homestead can last for generations.

INDEX

A

Adams, Shane and Kaity 151
Andrews, Joy 23

B

Barr, Thelma 65, 68, 105, 113
Beetch, Brad 108, 128, 131
Benson, David 87
Bradley, Dicky 128
Brand, Kenneth 40
Brand, Kenneth and Betty 84
Brimer, Brenda Wessner 145
Britnell, David 68
Brown, Gary 124
Brown, Rachel 113
Burns, Kyra 37, 131

C

Childers, Elizabeth 90
Childers, Louis 37, 83, 116
Childers, Martha 83
Clark, Bruce 15
Condra, Sylvia 34, 37, 64, 89
Crouch, Gene 64, 113
Cunningham, James 91

D

Davis, Diana 149
Deckleman, Celia 133, 135
Denton, Billy 44
Denton, Lynn 101
Dickson, Francis 18

E

Easterling, Travis 69, 70, 115
Eddleman, Travis 24, 108, 138
Ellis, John 136
Evans, Kathy 90

F

Fair, Wilford and Ellen 17
Fletcher, Gary 53
Forbis, Larry 61, 62
Forbis, Mike 61
Foust, Helen 58, 73
Foust, Jimmy 58, 73, 113
Frazey, Harry 78
Frazey, James 107
Furnatter, Katherine 111

INDEX

G

Goad, Lesley 84
Gustafson, Alyce 25, 31, 37, 87

H

Hammond, Sean and Cori 91
Heeb, Berneda 17, 33, 34, 68
Heeb, Brody 31
Heeb, Helen 150
Heeb, Jimmy 32
Heeb, Tony 131
Heeb, Wilma and Freda 137
Henderson, Mike 102
Hoenick, Lois 57
Hoenick, Tony 57
Hollan, Ed 48, 122
Holmes, James 36
Holmes, Mark 138
Hurd, Harlan 56

J

Jernigan, Steve 69, 94
Johns, Carrie 90
Jones, Estelle 34
Jones, Justin 147
Jones, Mitch 151
Jones, Randy 147, 150
Jones, Randy (Harrisburg) 38

K

Keller, Trey 54
Kelley, Jesse 50

L

Leder, Roger 53, 119, 126, 127, 134
Lovelace, Tom 77
Lovell, Captain 64

M

Mann, Margaret 34, 64
Mann, Milton 64

Marsh, Steve 50, 53, 54, 69, 101, 119, 127, 134, 138
Martinez, Nick 50, 53, 54, 101, 119, 134, 135
Mathews, Allen 93
McClain, Charlie 19, 27, 52, 101
McClain, Gary 107
McClain, Linda 52
McCrary, Collin 97
McDermott, John 44
McGee, Jimmie 34
Milam, Jerry Dan 77
Milam, Martha 89
Mooney, Matthew 147
Morgan, Mark 58
Morris, Barbara 126
Mross, Lexsi 65
Mross, Maddi 91
Murphy, Tim 106

P

Parker, Bertie Sue 100
Parker, Bob 38
Parker, Caroline 37, 52, 75, 81, 84, 85, 91, 97, 136
Parker, Henry 38
Parker, Jean 19, 50, 59
Parker, Kaiser 37
Parker, Matt 31
Parker, Ricky 113
Pilcher, Billy Wayne 29
Pilcher, Walter and Helen 21
Prescott, Marshallene 73

R

Reddmann, Annetta 92, 107, 150
Reddmann, Morgan 151
Redd, Mary Sue 116
Reeves, David 106
Roberts, Butch 62, 64
Roberts, John E. 18, 31, 44, 45, 64, 73, 128, 142, 143, 145
Roberts, Ruthie 34, 44, 128, 145

INDEX

Rolland, Pete 38, 79
Rosa, Tommye 18, 73, 93, 94, 96, 103, 115, 147
Rushing, Charlotte 121

S

Sadler, Butch and Krissy 148
Sadler, Genny 26, 36
Sadler, Mark 36, 39, 52, 148, 150
Sanders, Kyle 65
Sanders, Vivian 18, 34, 78
Shannon, Lucille Brunson 17
Sloan, Betty 111
Smith, J. C. 59
Smith, J.C 59, 60
Spears, Mary 73
Square Deal 47, 73
Steyer, Carl 39, 52, 101, 148, 150
Steyer, Martin 45
Sutton, John and Amber 148
Swanner, Wilburn 34

T

Tarkington, Clara 34
Tedder, Howard 27, 45
Thomas, John 56, 57
Thomas, Nathan 74, 75, 134, 135, 151
Tucker, Dakota 94
Tudor, C. Edward 15, 55, 56, 57, 60, 94

V

Vaughn, Travis 41, 43, 50, 51

W

Wallace, Arthur 73
Wallace, David 92
Wallace, John 92, 147
Wallace, Kim 147
Webb, Carl 36
Webb, Chuck 36, 101
Webb, Wanda 36
Wess, LaFarrell 34
Westlake, Marion 64
Whitmire, Mandy 107
Whitmire, Seth and Mandy 84, 151
Williams, Red 117
Wilson, Vaughn 50, 51, 52
Winningham, Don 107
Winningham, Jimmy 48
Winningham, Vickie 92, 150
Wolfe, Buck 79
Woodham, Carl 40, 106, 123
Woodham, Josie 73
Worley, Charlie 47, 105
Wright, Margie 61

Y

Young, Bob 45

ABOUT THE AUTHOR

Mary Anne Parker grew up in Fredericksburg, Texas, and relocated to Arkansas at age twenty. She studied history at Arkansas State University and met Cy Parker in the winter of 2000. The School Kids and festival of that year were her first events to work at Parker Homestead. Over the years, Mary Anne's Homestead duties have varied from selling sarsaparilla to parking cars, driving a four-wheeler to pull a trailer full of visitors to scaring the dickens out of Haunted Homestead visitors and playing trombone in the loft of the barn to making brooms. Probably her favorite Homestead job thus far has been preparing for and enjoying the Homestead holiday wine tasting event.

My family and I: (left to right) Caroline, Cy, Kaiser and me. *Photo by Nikki Morrow.*

Mary Anne married Cy in 2003, and they have two wonderful children: Caroline, fifteen, and Kaiser, six. They live in Whitehall with the Bacon Hotel in their front yard and the Homestead to the back, next door to Aunt

About the Author

T, down the road from Cy's niece Kyra and, if you venture just a bit further down Homestead Road, you will dead end at Phil and Teressa's house. It is a wonderful life.

Visit us at
www.historypress.net

This title is also available as an e-book